Praise for Susan Campbell's
Saying What's Real

"Compassionate, easily accessible, and profoundly practical, *Saying What's Real* is a wonderful resource for all who wish to experience successful communication and the intimacy that results from truly understanding each other."

— Sue Patton Thoele, author of *The Courage to Be Yourself, Growing Hope,* and *The Woman's Book of Soul*

"In *Saying What's Real,* Susan Campbell offers her readers an executive summary for good communication. The seven phrases are simple and effective — employ them and your relationships will undoubtedly improve."

— Jett Psaris, PhD, coauthor of *Undefended Love*

"There is no book I have ever come across that so cleanly, clearly, and simply outlines the skills that will allow you to truly hear your partner and be heard. If you want rich and healing communications in your relationship, this is the book for you."

— Mary O'Malley, author of *The Gift of Our Compulsions*

"*Saying What's Real* is the clearest and most useful guide to successful relating imaginable! If everyone practiced these key communication strategies there would be much more happiness and many fewer divorces!"

— Deborah Anapol, PhD,

author of *Polyamor*

SAYING WHAT'S
REAL

Other books by Susan Campbell, PhD

Truth in Dating

Getting Real

Beyond the Power Struggle

The Couple's Journey

Earth Community

Expanding Your Teaching Potential

From Chaos to Confidence

The Everything Great Sex Book
(coauthored with Suzie Heumann)

SAYING WHAT'S
REAL

7 KEYS TO AUTHENTIC COMMUNICATION

AND RELATIONSHIP SUCCESS

SUSAN CAMPBELL, PhD

AUTHOR OF *GETTING REAL*

An H J Kramer Book

published in a joint venture with

New World Library

An H J Kramer Book

published in a joint venture with

New World Library

Editorial office:
P.O. Box 1082
Tiburon, California 94920

Administrative office:
14 Pamaron Way
Novato, California 94949

Cover design by Bill Mifsud
Text design and typography by Tona Pearce Myers

Library of Congress Cataloging-in-Publication Data
Campbell, Susan M., 1941–
  Saying what's real : seven keys to authentic communication and relationship success / Susan M. Campbell.— 1st ed.
      p.   cm.
Includes bibliographical references and index.
ISBN 1-932073-12-4 (pbk. : alk. paper)
1. Interpersonal communication. I. Title.
BF637.C45C33 2005
158.2—dc22   2004021299

First printing, February 2005
ISBN 1-932073-12-4
Printed in Canada on acid-free, partially recycled paper
Distributed to the trade by Publishers Group West

10 9 8 7 6 5 4 3 2 1

For my mother who, at 93, is still one of the most present, open, and real people I know.

CONTENTS

FOREWORD

Over the years I have read dozens of books about relationships hoping to better understand and improve my own relationships. Apparently, many other people have done the same thing, and I am not alone in this quest for insight. The plethora of relationship books being published today points to a real need for these books. At best, relationship issues are difficult. And as our awareness of gender equality and relationship roles has grown and changed, these issues have become more and more challenging.

I first became aware of Susan Campbell's pioneering work through her book *The Couple's Journey*. Of the many books on relationships I had read, this was the only one that squarely addressed the issues of longevity and full equality. It changed my whole understanding of what it takes to be successful in a long-term, committed relationship. Susan's approach to relationships informed and improved my own work on personal growth. I have since become an avid follower of her work.

Today she is an acknowledged leader in relationship consciousness. With her most recent book, *Truth in Dating,* and the reality TV show (based on her book) that she moderates, Susan has further broadened her influence, sharing her relationship expertise and encouraging relationship intimacy to a continuously growing audience. When Susan asked me to write the foreword to her new book, I immediately accepted this opportunity to turn more people on to her work.

Saying What's Real: Seven Keys to Authentic Communication and Relationship Success is an excellent resource for our new collective consciousness on how to thrive as humans and create true love through honesty in all our relationships.

Honesty is not easy. The famous studies done by Hugh Hartshorne and Mark May in the early 1930s showed clearly that everyone cheats and lies a little. Part of our dishonesty is unconscious. Many of us have repressed our true feelings, wants, and beliefs for so long that we do not know what is truly real about ourselves. It takes hard work, a willingness to be rigorously honest, and a belief that the truth will set us free to give our real selves a new birth.

Being your honest self is a challenge, and Susan's seven keys in *Saying What's Real* are excellent tools to help you communicate more honestly. To change, we have to take action. The tools provided in this book will unequivocally help you to discover your true reality so that you can say what you really feel, want, and believe. At the same time, the keys will help you achieve a new level of connectedness with your significant other and with others in your life.

An honest transformation will take place, perhaps not instantly, but certainly over time. Intimacy is impossible without honesty, and honesty will reveal each person's uniqueness. Even if your partner does not use these tools, your relationship will become more honest and real if you use them because it will allow your partner to know the real you.

What I like most about this book is its call for us to learn about and enjoy each other's differences. When we are in touch with what is real in ourselves and are willing to express it, others will necessarily see that our feelings, wants, and beliefs are not always the same as their feelings, wants, and beliefs. In fact, sometimes they are radically different.

Susan urges us to "hold differences" — a rather advanced communication practice but one that anyone can learn by reading the examples in the chapters that follow. I wholeheartedly encourage you to read this book and learn its lessons by practicing them. Then, we, like the French, can say "vive la différence." We can begin to celebrate our unique qualities and the differences between ourselves and others as we communicate more honestly in our relationships. You now hold in your hands the keys to relationship success.

— John Bradshaw
September 2004

INTRODUCTION
AN INVITATION TO CONSCIOUS COMMUNICATION

Communication between people is a multilayered process. Because of this fact, many of us feel inadequate in our attempts to understand others and be understood. Whenever any two people try to communicate, there are at least two levels to that communication: the overt, conscious message and the covert, hidden message. The overt message consists of the words we hear and the gestures we see. The hidden message has more to do with the intent behind the words. This is something we ordinarily overlook because we don't have the language to deal with it. Consider this example: on her way out the door, Jerry's seventeen-year-old daughter Melanie announces, "Don't wait up. I'll probably be home after midnight." The overt message here is some information about what time she'll be home. What's the hidden message? She is telling him that she is making her own decisions now about what time she'll get home. She's letting him know that he no longer has that sort of power over her. In other words, she's asserting her independence.

Jerry receives and registers his daughter's message on both levels. He hears her words. And he feels a discomfort in his gut — there's something about her statement that just does not sit well with him. But, like most people, Jerry has not been trained to put value on his subtler gut-level reactions. So he nods robotically and gives his usual reply: "Have a good time and be careful."

A communication like this leaves both people with a sense of incompleteness. There's something between them that has not been acknowledged. The next time they are together, that unfinished business will affect how relaxed and connected they feel with each other. In time, as more and more of these incomplete communications recur, their communication channels will become more clogged.

If Jerry had better communication skills, he might notice the uneasy feeling in his gut and comment on it instead of going on automatic. Even if he didn't know why, he'd still trust his gut feeling that there was more to Melanie's message than the words he heard. If Jerry had access to the Seven Keys to Authentic Communication and Relationship Success that you'll learn about in the following chapters, he might respond, "Hearing you say that, I feel uncomfortable. Are you telling me that you're now setting your own curfew?" Or he might feel something stronger, such as anger: "Hearing you say you'll be home after midnight, I feel angry. I think we need to talk more about this."

Using the key phrase, "Hearing you say that, I feel..." gives Jerry a lead-in to stay present to his feelings and thoughts about what he just heard. It helps him pay attention to his more deeply felt but subtler reactions, enabling him to respond in a more authentic way.

In this book, you will learn about how and when to use this key phrase and six others to make yourself a more authentic, conscious, and powerful communicator. These phrases support you in noticing and expressing what you really feel — so you'll be more effective in your relationships with others.

Cleaner Communication Equals Less Stress

We all know how unclear communication and unfinished business from the past interferes with our ability to be present. Knowing the seven keys helps you prevent the buildup of unfinished business in your communications with mates, lovers, friends, family, and coworkers. These tools help you get in touch with what you are feeling and express it rather than stuff it. Some of these tools can also be useful for cleaning up old business from the past.

Unclear communications and unexpressed discomfort about them are a major source of stress in our lives. How often have you wasted energy worrying about what you should have said or wondering what someone really meant? Imagine how much more time and energy we'd all have if we had better communication skills.

The seven keys help you become more present — so they could also be seen as seven keys to present-centered relating.

When your communications are based on present-time feelings, and you know how to skillfully clean up the old business from your past, you have a lot more of your mental attention and energy available to you.

Unmasking the Intent to Control

In my opening paragraph I mentioned that every communication has an intent behind it. Most of us do not have the knowledge, the skill, or the confidence to address the often hidden intent of another's communication — especially if the intent has something to do with trying to control an unknown outcome or trying to mask one's anxiety about feeling "not in control." People try to manipulate the outcome of their interactions all the time. And if they're not doing that, they're trying to bolster their egos by acting more in control or "on top of" the situation than is actually the case. In my research, I discovered that almost 90 percent of all human communication comes from the (usually unconscious) intent to control. Most of us are not aware of when we are communicating with the intent to control and when we are expressing our feelings and thoughts simply to exchange feelings or information.

> Almost 90 percent of all human communication comes from the (usually unconscious) intent to control.

The intent to control reveals itself in many disguises:

- denying that you feel pain when you're hurting
- trying to impress others
- manipulating to get what you want

- being nice or agreeable to avoid a hassle
- lying to protect someone's feelings
- assuming you know something that you really cannot know, instead of living with the uncertainty of the situation (e.g., jumping to conclusions or making assumptions about what someone else's behavior means)
- keeping silent to avoid conflict
- playing it safe
- trying not to rock the boat
- trying to appear more "together" or composed than you really feel

As you look down this list, you'll notice that all of these things have something to do with avoiding uncomfortable feelings (e.g., anxiety about feeling not in control) or avoiding an unwanted outcome. Perhaps you recognize yourself in one or more of these examples. If you do, then you're probably aware enough to admit that this sort of controlling doesn't really work. We may cling to the illusion of control and continue trying to predict or manipulate the outcome — for example, we may try to make ourselves feel more comfortable by assuming we know how someone else is going to react to us. But we can't; such things are unknowable until they are revealed in time. If you are focused more on avoiding the discomfort of not knowing than on communicating and really listening to others, you are not present. You're in your head or in the future — as if you're playing a game of chess: "If I make this move, my opponent will have to make that move." This is an example of the intent to control. This sort of strategizing keeps you in a state of chronic fear or anxiety. Trying to avoid uncertainty is very stressful. On the other hand, when you relax your grip, allow things to unfold, and pay attention to what is actually going on (vs. your wishful thinking or your fears), you are naturally more confident.

Again, most people are not even conscious of the fact that most of their self-talk and communication with others comes from the intent to control. It's no wonder that they often feel frustrated and out of control. You see, the more you try to control things, the more out of control you feel. When you are more focused on creating a favorable outcome or a favorable impression than on expressing yourself authentically, you are reinforcing your fears and anxieties.

> **The more you try to control things, the more out of control you feel.**

You are in a sense affirming that if things do not turn out according to plan, you will not be okay. This puts your well-being on pretty shaky ground. The fact is, you will be okay. And the only way to really discover this and learn to trust yourself is to risk feeling what you feel and expressing yourself authentically. Feeling and expressing what's so for you in each moment is what I call "getting real," or "relating." There is a big difference between communication that comes from the intent to relate and communication that comes from the intent to control.

Controlling Is Largely Unconscious

Most people's communications are tarnished by unconscious defense mechanisms designed to protect them from feeling hurt, rejected, abandoned, controlled, or not in control. All of us have been hurt by other people at some time in our lives as we have tried to express ourselves authentically, offer love, or get our needs met. Somewhere in our past we learned various strategies to protect ourselves in order to minimize further damage. In my own case, I learned to judge my father for how easily he was provoked to anger rather than simply feel my fear of his anger at me. So now, when someone I love gets angry at me, I have a tendency to judge rather than feel. Most of us have developed similar control patterns, and we're not even conscious of how this robs us of our ability to feel and express our real feelings. We may not be conscious of our patterns, but other people are impacted by them nonetheless. And we are impacted when we're on the receiving end of such strategies — as we saw in the case of Jerry and Melanie.

But healthy human communication is not really about protecting ourselves from discomfort or controlling how others react to us. Healthy communication, communication that fosters connection, trust, intimacy, and respect, is about *knowing and being known*. It is not about getting people to do what we want. It's about creating mutually beneficial solutions. It is not about controlling what we feel. It is about feeling what we feel, and sharing what we feel and think in the present moment. This sort of openhearted sharing is "relating."

> Healthy human communication is not really about protecting ourselves from discomfort or controlling how others react to us. Healthy communication, communication that fosters connection, trust, intimacy, and respect, is about *knowing and being known*.

Controlling vs. Relating: What's the Difference?

Here is an example of how the intent to control might show up subtly in an intimate relationship. Georgia tells her husband, "Since you're going out with your friends tonight, I think I'll call my ex and see if he wants to come over. He still enjoys my company." Instead of telling her husband how she feels about his going out without her, she sends the not-so-subtle message that if he chooses not to be with her this evening, she'll find someone else who will. If her husband, Howie, knew how to say what's real, he would reply, "Hearing you say that, I feel..." (followed by a feeling such as *disappointed, threatened, angry,* or *insecure).* Without such tools, he'll probably do what most unskilled communicators would do — he'll try to act unruffled or in control: "Sure, honey... whatever." The phrase "Hearing you say that, I feel..." supports relating. Most people are in the habit of controlling.

This phrase helps you bring your awareness to this present moment. When you can do this, you're more connected to yourself and to the overall context, so you feel more confident and powerful. Fear of an unwanted outcome recedes into the background and is replaced by trust, the most basic kind of trust there is — the trust that no matter what the outcome, you will be resourceful enough to deal with it.

The Seven Keys Help You Feel Safe

The seven key phrases you are about to learn are designed to enhance your capacity for love and trust by bringing your awareness into this present moment. The regular use of these seven statements proves that when you know how to focus your attention on the present moment of contact instead of getting caught up in the mind's machinations and strategies, you naturally feel safe. You learn that you don't need to insure a predictable outcome to feel okay. Then you can let go of the illusion of control.

> The seven key phrases are designed to enhance your capacity for love and trust by bringing your awareness into this present moment. When you know how to focus your attention on the present moment of contact, you naturally feel safe.

On the other hand, if you allow your attention to be clouded by hidden agendas and unfinished business that you do not know how to address, you will feel unsafe. When you feel unsafe, your need to control things gets magnified. This breeds further fear and mistrust.

It has taken me thirty-five years of working as a relationship coach and teamwork consultant to boil the knotty problem of human communication down to its essence. The seven statements you are about to learn are essential for having authentic relationships. Use them whenever you want to keep your attention focused on what is going on here and now with this person in front of you. Using these seven statements prevents your fears about an uncertain outcome from taking over because you are more connected to yourself and to the other in present time. Feeling present and connected keeps your attention on what you're doing. This is very empowering. When you're present, you're not in fear. Fear is about the future.

The need to control the outcome often comes from the fear that something will happen in the future that you won't be able to deal with, so you try to control how you come across or how the other person responds to you. Present-centered communication (relating) is open and relaxed about such things. Your aim is to express yourself authentically and allow the other to have whatever reaction he has. When you are not so focused on controlling the outcome or your anxiety about the outcome, your attention is available to deal with what's really going on right here in front of you. You're naturally going to be more resourceful.

When you're present, you're not in fear. Fear is about the future.

Take Jerry and Melanie's brief conversation as a case in point. If Jerry had told her, "Hearing you say I shouldn't wait up for you, I'm feeling uncomfortable," he would have made real contact and received his daughter's attention in a more meaningful way.

Using the seven key phrases brings you into a frame of mind that taps into your natural loving and self-trusting *essence,* as opposed to your self-protective (fear-based) *conditioned self.* You develop the ability to relate more and control less. And you learn that whatever the other's reaction, you'll find within yourself the resources to deal with it.

Can You Make These Statements?

Before being introduced to the Seven Keys to Relationship Success, take the following quiz. The quiz consists of fifteen statements, not seven. But all fifteen are variations on the seven, and when applied consistently they can lead to successful outcomes for most relationship dilemmas.

Take a look at the fifteen statements below. Next to each statement, write 0 if it would rarely or never occur to you to say this, 1 if you might occasionally make this statement, and 2 if such a statement is typical of your style.

1. Hearing you say how that affected you, I feel sorry I did that.

2. I want you to listen and hear me out before responding.

3. I'm sorry. If I had it to do over, I would...

4. Tell me more about why you feel/think/see it that way.

5. I didn't mean to hurt you. What I wish I'd been able to communicate is...

6. I'd like to make it up to you/to make amends.

7. Could we sit down and talk about something that's on my mind?

8. I'm feeling unfinished about that recent conversation between us. Could we talk about it?

9. I need some time before I respond to you.

10. I see it differently than that. May I tell you how I see it?

11. I think/favor/want... What do you think/favor/want?

12. I appreciate you for... (something this person did or said).

13. I want... How does that work for you? (Is this something you can give?)

14. I feel crummy about what just happened. Can we talk about it?

15. I notice myself getting defensive. I think I'm getting triggered.

SCORING

The highest possible score is thirty, and the lowest would be zero. The higher your score, the higher your likelihood of having successful relationships. Here is a breakdown of what your scores might mean:

- 0–9: You probably find yourself frustrated in relationships more often than you would like. This book will open your eyes to new possibilities.

- 10–15: You have a high aptitude for relating and are open to learning. You will probably find the skills and tools in this book compatible with your style.

- 16–24: You have good relationship skills and have the aptitude to take your skills to the highest level if you wish. Read on!

- 25–30: Your capacity for present-centered relating is already at a very high level. Congratulations! Perhaps this book can be useful in helping others you know reach the level you're already at.

Benefits You Can Expect

If you are like most people, you need to believe there is a reasonable chance of succeeding before trying something new in potentially risky situations. The seven key phrases foster greater self-confidence when you're trying something new because they give you an actual script to get you started. Once you have uttered the words, "Hearing you say that, I feel...," the rest is a lot easier.

Other benefits you can expect are:

- *The seven keys bring you into the here and now.* This helps you stay focused on what is real rather than what is imagined or feared. Fears are usually about the future. When you are present, you are in your body and more apt to be in your heart as well. This helps others trust you more and helps you trust yourself.

- *They make you more resourceful.* When you are more conscious and present, you are more resourceful. Your attention is on your current reality, so your communications are more likely to bring successful outcomes.

- *They make your communication more impactful.* When you make stronger, more intimate contact, you are more likely to get the other's full attention. You are not easy to ignore.

- *They put you in a more open state of mind* by helping you access a fuller range of feelings, including the softer feelings and wants that lie underneath the harder, more defensive feelings. This builds empathy, trust, and rapport between yourself and others.

- *They assist you in feeling connected* not just with yourself and the other, but also with your entire context or current reality. This means your communications are more apt to be appropriate to the situation rather than understated or over the top. When you are more connected to your current reality, you make healthier choices because you see more of the total picture.

- *They put you and the other person into a cooperative relationship* rather than an adversarial one. When you communicate with the intent to relate using these statements, you are sending the meta-message, "I'm on your side, I value this relationship, I'm willing to take a risk or take some leadership to help make our relationship better."

- *They help you unhook from who you think you are or who you think you should be.* Being in the present and communicating from that experience of presence allows you to expand your identity to one that is more spiritually unified with all that is. When you're not focused on controlling the outcome, you tend to feel mostly loving, relaxed, and open — even when things don't go your way. Presence brings you into a state of harmony and unity with the rest of life. When you are simply authentically present, you tend to become less invested in your self-image or who you think you are.

Communicating with Awareness

Practicing the seven keys is a curriculum for presence. They foster a high level of self-awareness in each moment. This engenders respect and openness from others, whereas trying to *make* others respect you engenders the opposite.

They remind you to *relate*. When you are relating, your communications take on a quality of caring, openness, and authenticity that just naturally engenders respect and love. It's a paradox — when you stop trying to play it safe or get others' approval, then you wind up winning the admiration and respect you want. When you are trying to control the outcome, you are in your head, imagining something that is not now. Your communications tend to come across as less connected, less genuine, and therefore less trustworthy. People may feel manipulated around you without knowing why.

> When you stop trying to play it safe or get others' approval, then you wind up winning the admiration and respect you want.

Whenever you are in a situation where you can't get through to someone or communications have hit a wall, try using one of these seven key phrases. If one doesn't work for you, try another. In most difficult situations, any one of the seven can get things moving again because they all bring you into present time. In a very real sense, they bring you back to reality.

Sometimes using just one of these phrases will get you back on track or keep you on the right course. Other times, you'll want to use two or more of them together.

In the chapters that follow, you'll be learning about how and when to apply these seven vital communication practices.

SAYING WHAT'S
REAL

1

HEARING YOU SAY THAT, I FEEL...

Hearing you say that, I feel relieved.
Hearing you say that, I feel hurt.
Hearing you say you want me to come over tonight,
I'm feeling afraid to disappoint you.
Hearing you say you felt neglected, I'm thinking, "I wish I'd
been there when you got home from the emergency room."

Telling someone how you feel after he or she expresses
something important builds intimacy and connection.
Most of us have a somewhat limited vocabulary when
it comes to expressing our in-the-moment feelings, so we are
more likely to offer an automatic or habitual response than to
connect heart-to-heart. We're more likely to explain or defend ourselves when someone expresses anger, rather than letting the other know how we feel hearing her displeasure with
us. Or when someone gives us a compliment, we're more apt
to reply with a quick comeback, rather than openly receiving
and registering that person's words.

Your mate tells you he's going to a meeting tonight when
you'd been hoping for an intimate evening together. You feel
disappointed, but instead of revealing this in a way that allows
him to see you and feel you, you come back with, "You always

Most of us have a somewhat limited vocabulary when it comes to expressing our in-the-moment feelings, so we are more likely to offer an automatic or habitual response than to connect heart-to-heart.

need to be on the go, don't you?" Then you complain about "not feeling heard" or "not being seen."

Your son comes home from school bragging about how well he did on an exam. You continue doing whatever you had been doing and, without looking up, reply: "That's great," or some other stereotypical response. What if instead you connected with him on a feeling level? "Hearing that you scored at the 90th percentile, I feel so proud of you!"

Your mate tells you about a tough interaction she had at work. In an attempt to be supportive, you automatically go into "fix it" mode, offering ideas about how she might have handled it differently. What if instead, you simply responded, "Hearing you say your coworker went over your head again, I feel upset. I'm really glad you're talking to me about it"?

Revealing feelings the moment they are occurring is a rather advanced communication practice. It's an option that simply does not occur to most people because most of us grew up in families where people ignored one another's essential humanness. Most of us long to be seen, heard, and felt by those closest to us, but we learned a long time ago to settle for less, suffer in silence, and carry around a lot of unhealed pain and resentment. If we could all learn how to respond on a feeling level to each other, our adult relationships could be a source of tremendous healing. Couples who have worked with me, for example, report that learning how to connect with feelings using the seven keys has shown them how to satisfy each other's unmet childhood longings in their current relationship.

Healing Childhood Wounds

As a longtime couples counselor, I have found that most couples enter marriage with the unconscious agenda of healing themselves through their relationship. At some level we know we have been emotionally wounded due to the insensitivity of our early caregivers. Most of these caregivers were well-intentioned but had little training or guidance in responding to human emotions.

It's not too late to transform our adult relationships into vehicles for healing the past. The way to do this is to practice the language of feelings. To assist you in identifying your feelings, take a look at the list of feelings and sensations below — noting which ones you have an easy time expressing and which are difficult or foreign to you. As you read through the feelings list, imagine yourself using the phrase "Hearing you say that, I feel..." followed by each emotion or sensation on the list. Notice how your body feels as you express these various feeling words. Notice your emotional tone as you report various sensations.

> Most couples enter marriage with the unconscious agenda of healing themselves through their relationship.

FEELINGS

I feel anger or I'm angry at you for... (something specific that the other said or did)

I feel sad

I feel disappointed

I feel happy

I feel appreciative

I feel resentful

I feel hurt

I feel upset

I feel numb, frozen, shut down

I feel anxious, uneasy, nervous

I feel expansive

I feel furious

I feel awed

I feel afraid

I feel shocked, stunned

I feel curious, open

SENSATIONS

I feel heat, cold

I sense tension (in my eyes, face, jaw, hands)

I sense contraction in my body

I sense relaxation in my body

I feel warm (in my belly, my heart, my face)

I feel agitation

I feel excitement

I feel nauseated

How We Learn to Ignore Feelings

People experience sensations and feelings all the time, but they may have learned not to pay attention to their inner world. As a youngster Jim felt pain when his mother directed or corrected him using a harsh tone of voice. He learned that it was less painful to simply tune her out and turn off his feelings, so he got into the habit of saying "Okeydokey" as his automatic response. Now as an adult married to Janine, when his wife asks him to do something that he has not already thought of, he takes it as a criticism, goes on automatic, and replies, "Okeydokey." Such a response communicates to Janine that he is not paying attention, and she gets louder and more strident in an attempt to connect. Jim feels resentful, but appears stoic.

What if he could let her know that her tone bothered him? What if he told her, "Hearing you say I need to paint the door in that tone of voice, I feel irritated"? This statement might not be pleasant for Janine to hear, but she would know that he was paying attention. She'd feel more connected and less abandoned, and she might even become more aware of her tone of voice.

Dealing with Unconscious Reactions

Some people feel hurt or angry and don't even realize it. Mary's husband Bruce tells her, "I'm going to bed now." Mary feels disappointed. She was hoping for a longer evening together. But does she tell Bruce this? No, her fear-of-rejection button has been triggered so she goes on automatic: "You're always so tired! We need to get you to a doctor." She avoids her own feelings and instead makes it his problem ("You're always so tired"). Instead of saying "I want...," she uses the more impersonal and safe form, "we need to." And she creates even more distance from him and from her own truth by generalizing about him ("you're always...").

What if she told Bruce, "Hearing you say that, I feel hurt. I'm thinking to myself that maybe you don't care about me as much as I care about you"? Can you see how this might lead to a more sensitive and real conversation? Hearing how she feels, he knows what's bothering her, so he can address it and perhaps reassure her that her fears are unfounded. Instead of accumulating more unfinished emotional business, they could clear the air and come back into the present with each other.

Using "Hearing you say that, I feel..." to frame your response keeps your communications responsible. You're taking responsibility for *what you feel,* not telling others *how they should be.* You're "staying on your own side of the net" — a metaphor for speaking only about what *you* experience rather than telling others how they feel or what *they* should be doing differently.

As long as she's talking about Bruce's tiredness, she's masking her real feelings. She's not talking about herself — she's over on his side of the net — making it *his* problem. Bruce feels mistrustful of her remark but isn't sure why. He senses that she's upset, but she hasn't given him anything real to respond to, so he says nothing and goes to bed with an uneasy feeling. They get up the next day feeling distant and cold toward each other.

If Mary knew how to respond with "Hearing you say that, I feel... hurt," she would have come across as more

> When you connect with your feelings, this instantly focuses your attention on what is real and present, which leaves a stronger, more palpable impression on others.

hear-able and feel-able to Bruce, more real and present. She is in her body, not in her head. She's making stronger contact. When you connect with your feelings, this instantly focuses your attention on what is real and present, which leaves a stronger, more palpable impression on others.

Mary is feeling hurt. Her hurt was triggered by her partner's actions. It is important to her relationship that she feel and express her upset and not avoid or repress it. Otherwise, she has no way to clear the air and no way to connect with Bruce in a genuine way. By revealing her pain, she is staying connected to Bruce. When she withholds or tries to bypass her feelings, this leads to feeling disconnected from him.

When you use this key phrase to help you embrace your pain voluntarily, there is a certain power and grace to that act. You are bringing the light of conscious awareness to your feelings and sensations. You are affirming that you are okay just as you are. Being present to pain is an act of self-affirmation and self-empowerment. You'll feel stronger and more resilient when you do this.

> When you use this key phrase to help you embrace your pain voluntarily, there is a certain power and grace to that act.

Enhancing Emotional Connection

Terrance says to Shayna, "You look pretty in that outfit." Shayna could come back with an automatic response like, "Well, I hope so. It cost enough!" Or she can respond on a feeling level, meeting his eyes with hers: "Hearing you say I look pretty, I feel pretty. I love it when you notice what I'm wearing." Again, can you see the difference between an automatic control pattern and a present-centered feeling response? Feelings offer the pair a chance to really connect, heart to heart.

In most interactions with loved ones, you have a choice between a reply that enhances intimacy and one that fosters superficiality or distance. Most people unconsciously choose the more superficial response. This dilutes the impact of their communications. Of course, there may be times when a more superficial comeback is appropriate; but if you want to build a strong bond with someone, stronger contact is usually the better choice.

> You have a choice between a reply that enhances intimacy and one that fosters superficiality or distance. Most people unconsciously choose the more superficial response. This dilutes the impact of their communications.

Learning to Flow with Change

One reason people avoid expressing uncomfortable feelings is they assume that by expressing a feeling, they are giving it too much importance. In actual fact, the opposite is true. If you express a painful feeling, shining the light of awareness on it, it's likely to become *less* prominent in your attention, not *more.* It becomes easier to let it go. It is when you keep your thoughts and feelings hidden from view that they persist and become magnified in your mind.

In my workshops, there are moments when two people are beginning to engage in dialogue and then one or both will quickly escape from genuine, perhaps uncomfortable, contact by going into a generalization or a story only remotely related to the here and now. That's when I try to bring them back into present time using this key phrase. I'll ask Partner A to state a feeling he is experiencing in relation to Partner B. Then, before B can escape into a story or a theory, I request that B simply pause, take in what A shared, check in with herself to see what she is experiencing right now, and then respond with, "Hearing you say that, I feel...." Then A does the same thing — listens, pauses, notices his feelings, and responds. When partners do this for a while, it's amazing to see how feelings can deepen and how the sense of connection can grow, simply by staying in the ever-changing present moment.

So besides keeping partners present and increasing their emotional contact, another benefit of this exercise is that it shows how easily feelings can change from moment to moment. If you give yourself the space to feel and express *what is* now, *what is* in the next moment will usually be different. In addition to helping people learn to be more comfortable with highly charged feelings, this exercise also helps them learn to trust that when they become conscious of and express a once-hidden feeling, that feeling is likely to change or transform.

Facing Up to Conflict

If you are feeling angry at someone for something he has just done or said, using this key phrase can give you a safe structure for expressing it. It helps you move past any temptation you may have to minimize or avoid conflict. The reason most people avoid conflict is they don't trust themselves to deal with their differences constructively. They fear doing damage to their relationships.

In my couples counseling work, I teach couples to fight fairly. The process begins with one person expressing a "beef." A beef is something you're not happy about, stated as something your partner did that triggered you and what your reaction was: "When you_____, I felt_____." Then I will instruct the other partner to reply with "Hearing you say that, I feel...." This keeps the listener from going into an explanation or a defensive reaction. After this the partner with the beef is instructed to reply using "Hearing you say that, I feel...." Then partners keep going back and forth like this, beginning with the phrase "Hearing you say that..." for a few minutes. As they do this, they discover that simply sharing one's feelings about what the other person just said can be immensely healing. Here is an example:

> Using this key phrase can give you a safe structure for expressing disagreement. It helps you move past any temptation you may have to minimize or avoid your differences.

JORGE: I have a beef to clear with you about the number of times you have started to talk before I'm finished. I felt irritated when you said, "Wait a minute, that's not quite it!" while I was telling Tom and Margie about how we got such a good deal on our new car.

PATRICE: Hearing you say that, I feel angry.

JORGE: Hearing you say that, I feel cold toward you.

PATRICE: Hearing you say that, I feel afraid.

JORGE: Hearing you say that, I feel connected to you.

PATRICE: Hearing you say that, I feel relief.

JORGE: Hearing you say that, I feel soft toward you.

PATRICE: Hearing you say that, I feel soft toward you and sorry that I said, "Wait a minute."

JORGE: Hearing you say that, I feel appreciation, and I feel forgiving toward you.

PATRICE: Hearing you say that, I feel grateful — grateful for your forgiveness and grateful to you for telling me about your beef.

JORGE: Hearing you say that, I feel complete. I feel open and loving toward you.

It can be tempting to react to someone's anger with a counterattack or an explanation rather than a feeling. But if partners will agree to use this simple phrase, they'll avoid the all-too-human tendency to become defensive or long-winded. Defensiveness and long-winded explanations dilute the quality and potency of your contact. These are examples of *controlling,* not relating. The key phrase "Hearing you say that, I feel . . ." is a discipline to keep you *relating* to each other.

I always feel moved as I witness two people listening, really checking in with themselves, and then sharing feelings. I can feel their tentativeness, their excitement, their aliveness. It's not easy to stay within this structure for such a long time, but the results are worth it.

> It can be tempting to react to someone's anger with a counterattack or an explanation rather than a feeling.

DO TRY THIS AT HOME

Ask someone you know to try this exercise with you. Sit face-to-face. Notice what you are feeling. Take turns speaking about how you are feeling right now about this relationship. In responding to the other, express your feelings about what was just said to you, beginning with the phrase, "Hearing you say that, I feel. . . ." Respond only to what you just heard and what you now feel after hearing this. Once you have expressed yourself, notice what you feel now. If you notice that your feelings have changed after you have expressed them, remember that this is natural. Try not to get stuck in the idea that you should remain "consistent" in your feelings. Feelings change after being expressed.

Allow the conversation to be completely spontaneous. Both people should be open to being surprised, not just by the other, but by themselves as well. When partners do this exercise, using the phrase "Hearing you . . ." as "training wheels," their communications tend to arise from a deeper level of their being, showing that you can let go of the need to explain or defend, be uncertain of where you are going, and still radiate confidence.

In these moments of heightened spontaneity, people embody a sense of confidence or self-trust that I rarely see in their more controlled personas. The willingness to just share feelings with another person, without trying to control the outcome, opens up vast new possibilities. As we learn to trust the outcome without trying to control it, we learn to be more generally trusting of the unknown and the chaotic. Trusting yourself to handle unknown outcomes is a very valuable life skill.

Staying Open to New Possibilities

The key phrase "Hearing you say that..." helps you slow down and pay attention to what's bubbling up in your awareness right now. It keeps you from resorting to habitual or scripted comebacks. And it helps you stay in touch with the fact that you cannot know what's coming next, but you can prepare yourself to stay present to whatever happens. Being in an open, nondefensive frame of mind is the best preparation for dealing with life as it comes. Remember, when you're feeling uncertain or unsure about what's coming next, you can be pretty sure that you're in touch with present-time reality. Being in present time together is what makes an interaction come alive. To experience true intimacy, two people must be able to enter the unknown and the uncertain together. Partners who do this regularly report that this keeps their relationships vital, growing, and juicy.

> To experience true intimacy, two people must be able to enter the unknown together.

Thoughts Are Worth Sharing, Too

Sometimes it is a thought that needs to be shared rather than a feeling. Or sometimes it's both. If my partner has just told me he wants to invest a large sum of money in new equipment, I might respond with, "Hearing you say you want to buy that new system, I'm thinking, 'What's wrong with the system we have?'" Sharing thoughts by quoting your in-the-moment self-talk is more self-revealing and relational than if you only came back with, "What's wrong with the system we have?" Can you see the difference? Sharing a thought as a *disclosure* of the actual words or sentences going on in your head is a lot friendlier than the more challenging and perhaps aggressive comeback, "What's wrong with what we have?"

If I were to share a feeling and then add my self-talk, my communication would be even more effective. It might look like this: "Hearing you say you want to buy that new system, I feel hesitant... and fearful. My self-talk is, 'What's wrong with the system we have?'" I have found that expressing your feeling first, and then your self-talk, is often a winning combination. Your feeling statement gets you emotionally connected to yourself and to the other, and your self-talk adds a bit more information about what's behind the feeling.

An especially good time to use this combination is when you and another disagree about something. It builds rapport and keeps you from reacting defensively or impulsively. It helps you stay present to your bodily sensations, so you'll feel more trusting, less fearful, and more heart-connected to the other person.

This Statement Builds Rapport

Whenever you reveal how you are affected by someone's words, this builds rapport, and the other person tends to trust you more.

Whenever you reveal how you are affected by someone's words, this builds rapport, and the other person tends to trust you more. People are more open to what you have to say because you have shown yourself to be open to them. Also, by stating feelings and self-talk before getting into the issue itself, you're connecting on a human level first.

What If the Other Overreacts?

Using this key phrase usually facilitates trust and openness. But what if you stay on your own side of the net and remain grounded in your feelings and the other misreads your intent and overreacts or jumps to the wrong conclusion? Then, you would need to employ "Hearing you say that..." again with whatever your present feeling is in this moment. For example, let's imagine my partner gets triggered or angry when I share my self-talk — "I'm thinking to myself, what's wrong with what we have?" — and replies, "You're always so fearful!" I might have the urge to jump over to his side of the net with, "You're not hearing me!"

If I could continue to use this key phrase to keep myself present, I'd reply, "Hearing you say that, I feel hurt," and then I would leave some silence. It's very important to allow silence after you state your feeling. Let your response sink in. Don't justify or apologize; justifying and explaining dilute your communication. Just remain respectfully silent and stay in contact. The ball is now in the other person's court. If I can stay present, there's a good chance he'll see that I am not behaving like an adversary. And maybe he'll become more present as well. It often works this way.

Using This Phrase to Heal a Damaged Relationship

Carl was a large, muscular man who wore his longish salt-and-pepper hair in a casual, loosely combed style and often went unshaven. He worked in a manufacturing plant next to a petite, well-groomed woman named Shirley. One day Shirley walked up to him and surprised him by saying, "I won't be working here from now on, starting tomorrow. I'm being moved to another department." When Carl asked why, Shirley told him that she had asked to be relocated because she had always felt afraid of him. Hearing this, Carl felt very hurt. Before taking my communication seminar, it would never have occurred to him to express his real feelings in a situation like this. ("Not a big guy like me!") His usual pattern would have been to come back with some quip like, "You don't need to be afraid of me, honey. I don't bite!" Such a statement might help him manage his own pain, but it would do nothing to bring him into present time or help Shirley see him more accurately.

In this instance, however, Carl was able to feel and express his true feelings. Instead of resorting to his usual control pattern, thus reinforcing her impression of him as insensitive and thick-skinned, he replied, "Hearing you say that you've always been afraid of me, I feel hurt." Then he remained silent and simply waited. After a few seconds, which seemed a lot longer than that, she told him softly, "I see that my words hurt you.... Now I see you in a different light.... You're not so tough...and I'm not afraid of you now. This is surprising." The next day Shirley informed him that she was not going to move to the other department after all. She had changed her mind about him.

Carl told me that this was a major turning point in his life. He had often been told by others that they were afraid or uncomfortable around him. It had never occurred to him to meet their remarks with anything other than defensiveness.

But now he had a way to really connect with people. What a discovery! He realized that it was a relief to reveal his vulnerable side instead of pretending to be so tough and cool about everything.

PRACTICING FEELINGS AND SELF-TALK

If you are lucky enough to have someone in your life who is willing to be your practice partner in a mutual journey to getting more present and real, invite this person to engage with you in the following skill practice. Sit or stand facing each other. Take a moment of silence to each identify one thing the other has done or said recently that created distance between the two of you — something that resulted in hurt feelings, anger, or mistrust. Then Person A starts by sharing what the other did that created distance: "When you_____, I felt_____." Person B listens and responds with, "Hearing you say that, I feel_____ and I'm saying to myself_____" (or *I'm thinking,* or *my self-talk is*_____). Then it is Person B's turn to share about the same question.

This exercise is a wonderful way to practice simply being present to another person's feelings without trying to fix anything. You'll discover that most of the time, just using this communication practice for expressing and being heard fixes things. With practice, you will learn that when two people shine the light of mutual consciousness on a troublesome situation, they experience that situation differently.

2 | I WANT...

I want to hear your feelings about what I'm saying.
I want to have a talk with you about something
I've had on my mind.
I want to feel your arms around me.
I want you to come with me to the store.
I want you to just listen and not say anything
until I'm finished.

In the previous chapter, we looked at how sharing feelings builds trust and fosters heart-to-heart connection. A want is a special type of feeling. You can usually feel a want in your body, and it often has an emotional tone to it. If you'd like more intimacy in your life, it's good to express your wants frequently and shamelessly.

Partnership is a place for giving and receiving attention, help, touch, and emotional nurturance. But because most of us did not get enough high-quality attention and nurturance as children, it's often difficult to stay in present time about our current wants. Based on early life experiences, we may have learned that expressing wants (or just *feeling* our wants) brings disappointment. So we carry the expectation into our present life that feeling and expressing wants leads to pain.

> Because most of us did not get enough high-quality attention and nurturance as children, it's often difficult to stay in present time about our current wants.

Having this unconscious negative expectation is one way to protect ourselves.

When you have unfinished emotional business from your past, it's hard to be open to the real possibilities of the present moment. Most of us recall a number of painful experiences where we asked for what we wanted and felt frustrated at the lack of response. This experience can lead to a pattern where you either overcommunicate or under-communicate your wants. Either you go over the top with demands, threats, or manipulations, or you minimize your wants by hinting, being indirect, accommodating, or giving up too soon. Does either of these patterns sound familiar to you? Can you see either of these tendencies in someone close to you?

The Time for Wants Is Now

The key phrase "I want..." coupled with a very specific statement of what it is you need, brings you into the here and now as you make a request. The aim of this phrase is to help you express a want that you are feeling in this very moment. It helps to interrupt any tendency you may have to make "announcements" about things that you need in general or forevermore. This is an important distinction: a here-and-now want is something you might actually be able to receive or not receive. An announcement about some generic want, such as "I want you to trust me more," is too general. It is not a request that can be met in this moment.

To be in present time with your wants, you would tell your partner, "I want you to look into my eyes," not "I want you to look at me *whenever* I'm speaking to you." In addition to the fact that the whenever phrase is less palpable, the word *whenever* also makes the whole statement sound more like a directive than a request. A directive is controlling. You're not making yourself vulnerable to receiving or not receiving in this moment. It is a general, once-and-for-all notification of a want. You're "putting the other person on notice" that from now on this is how he should treat you. The statement "I want you to look into my eyes" is specific to this moment. It comes from an actual *feeling* of wanting. The statement "I want you to look at me *whenever* I'm speaking" is not relational. It has a controlling flavor to it because it does not come from a present felt experience. It is more from the mind than from the heart — so the feeling tone is much different.

In recommending that you speak your in-the-moment wants, I am not saying that you should never make generic requests or directives. But the generic request is not so present and does not support stepping into the unknown with your partner. Real intimacy requires stepping into the unknown with someone — asking for what you want without trying to control the outcome.

A generic once-and-for-all request is usually a way to play it safe. You're trying to make sure your future needs will be met without your having to ask. When you are playing it safe, you are in a controlling stance. The once-and-for-all style of requesting is actually a control pattern. Remember, a control pattern is anything you do to avoid the anxiety of facing the unknown, the ambiguous, or the uncontrollable. Relating is present-time — allowing the future to be what it will be. The future is always unknown and uncontrollable. The best practice for learning to get comfortable with this fact of life is to feel any anxiety you may have about this rather than masking your anxiety with a control pattern. Anxiety about the unknown is normal. When you let go of trying to control things (including your own anxiety) and feel what you feel in the present, then your anxiety will diminish.

> Anxiety about the unknown is normal. When you let go of trying to control things (including your own anxiety) and feel what you feel in the present, then your anxiety will diminish.

Be Specific

Putting your requests in very specific terms lets the other know what type of help and nurturance work for you. A big mistake that many people make when asking for what they want is asking in a way that is so vague and general that the other person has no idea how to fulfill their request. They say, "I want you to be more reassuring." This is too general. Instead, I suggest saying, "I want you to tell me you're happy to see me." Likewise, instead of saying, "I want you to be more affectionate," tell your partner, "I like it when you come over and hug me when we're around the house together. I'd love a hug right now." Being specific is like painting a word picture that shows precisely what you want and how you want it. There is enough detail to help the other feel cared about and involved. The picture you paint shows you and your partner together, doing something satisfying or pleasurable. When you ask for what you want using specific language, it's more of a risk than when you ask for something using general terms. You're taking a risk on behalf of your relationship. You're putting yourself on the line. The other person will feel this and appreciate it.

Consider these additional examples of how to express your wants in specific terms:

- "I want you to find out what's playing at the movie theater and pick the film you most want to see and surprise me."

- "I love it when you hold my head in your hands and pull me toward you. Will you do that for me now?"

- "I want you to lie with me on the couch and put your arms around me."

Being specific brings both people into their bodies. It gives you a chance to kinesthetically try on having what you want. Making yourself present kinesthetically is a way of affirming your freedom to ask for whatever you are asking for.

Timing Is Critical

Besides being too vague or general, another mistake people make when expressing a want is asking for it at a time when it is unlikely to happen. Don't ask him to help you prepare dinner when he's studying for a final exam. Don't ask her to listen to the story of your

> Another mistake people make when expressing a want is asking for it at a time when it is unlikely to happen.

frustrating day when she is about to receive an important phone call. If you have had a long-standing want and just can't seem to get it satisfied, notice your timing. Are you asking for it at a time when you are actually feeling it? Or do you deliver a directive, as in, "I want more sex"? As I've demonstrated, generic requests do not have the same impact as asking for something at the very time you want it. "I'd like to make love with you this afternoon" has more impact than the generic, once-and-for-all "I want more sex."

The main reason a timely request has more impact is that your request is being made in present time. You are actually feeling your want, your vulnerability, and your openness to receive in this moment. There is an energetic connection between the two of you that your partner can feel. There is a real need occurring in you right now and a real possibility right now for your partner to act on your request (or not). You are taking a bigger risk. This gives your request more weight.

Poor Timing Can Be a Control Pattern

Some people make one or more of the above-mentioned mistakes because they really don't expect to get what they want anyway. So they sabotage themselves, secretly believing that they won't get their needs met no matter what they do. Being vague or using poor timing shields them from feeling the full impact of the disappointment and so this behavior is actually a control pattern to avoid pain. You are trying to protect yourself from experiencing the normal discomforts of life, or from feeling your real feelings. Self-sabotage is a control pattern because you are, in a sense, inflicting pain upon yourself before life can do it to you. It's as if you'd rather experience a pain that is certain and under your control than be open to the (uncertain) possibility of hearing a painful no (which is not within your control). Until you understand the cost of such defensive strategies, and begin to say what's real, you will never develop the self-trust you need to face the unknown with serenity.

Postponing Asking — Not a Good Idea!

Some people don't like to appear pushy, demanding, or needy, so they try to be very patient about their wants. As a result they wait to ask for what they want until there is a lot of pressure built up behind the want. In postponing their requests, they are trying to be nice or perhaps trying to appear "low maintenance." This strategy usually backfires because when you ask only infrequently, you are more likely to have expectations that the other should give you what you're asking for. (After all, you've been so accommodating!) Any time you have a lot of internal pressure behind a want, there will be a demanding or controlling tone to your request. Thus, what might have been an act

> It's better to ask whenever you feel a want rather than saving up and asking only for the really important things.

of transparent vulnerability turns into an expectation or a "should." (You've held off a long time on this need... haven't been asking for much... so the least your partner can do is grant this one tiny request!) The other person is likely to pick up your urgency and perhaps feel pressured or manipulated. The moral of this story is it's better to ask whenever you feel a want rather than saving up and asking only for the really important things.

Asking without Expectations

Expressing your in-the-moment wants, simply and directly, is a profound act of trust. As such, it helps you learn self-trust. Here's how that works: You are making a commitment to this moment, stepping into the unknown without knowing how the other will respond. You recognize that you may get what you want and you may not. By asking from an open-to-hearing-yes-or-no frame of mind, you are affirming both your right to ask and the other's right to refuse. And you are affirming that however things go, you will deal with it. It is very important that you do not unconsciously assume that you must have your want satisfied. This would be affirming the opposite — that you won't be okay unless the other says yes to your request.

Can you see how staying open, rather than being controlling, helps build your self-trust? When you allow for the possibility of not getting what you want, you are trusting yourself to deal with whatever happens. If your request does *not* feel like a step into the unknown, then maybe you have a belief that you should always get what you ask for. Check to see if your request contains the embedded message: "You'd better give me what I want, or there'll be trouble!" If you do believe that you must get what you ask for, do some self-inquiry about where this belief originated and what pain you're trying to avoid. For example, ask yourself when in the past you experienced so much pain about not getting what you wanted that you thought you might never recover. This would be the pain you are still trying to avoid.

Why Directives Lead to Disappointment

Here's another reason to be here now. Whenever you announce in advance a want that you expect the other to remember from this point forward, you are setting yourself up for disappointment. When Sheira tells Carlos, "I want you to help around the house more," she is giving a directive that she expects him to remember. If he's like most people, Carlos is not going to be thinking of his wife's need for help with housework on a daily basis. He'd do better if he heard her want at a time when she's feeling it and when he is free to say yes if he chooses to.

I have mentioned several reasons why generic directives do not work: the timing of the request is too distant from when the help might actually occur and so his experience of her need is not as palpable and has less impact. Even more significant than these reasons is the fact that putting someone on notice comes across as controlling. It's like giving someone marching orders rather than communicating a heartfelt need. Most people resist being controlled.

If people could say what they want more often, instead of making generic requests and holding secret expectations that the other is expected to divine, there would be less frustration and anger in the world. Much of our anger comes from suppressing our assertion — so we walk through life with unexpressed, and therefore unrequited, wants. Frustrated people are angry people. Let's help reduce the overall frustration level in the world by creating more favorable conditions for our wants to be heard and received.

Why We Don't Say What We Want

Some people are uncomfortable expressing wants because they imagine they'll appear demanding or controlling. ("What if I ask for what I want, and he sees me as a nag?") But my clients and I are discovering that expressing wants can be an act of transparency or vulnerability. It really depends on the intent. Are you asking in a way that *reveals* what you want? Or does your manner of asking *imply a threat* that if you don't get what you're asking for, there's going to be trouble? Asking in a way that reveals your self is an act of love. This is an example of the intent to *relate*. Asking in a way that implies a threat is aggressive and fear-inducing. This would be an example of the intent to *control*.

But even if you do get good at revealing your wants, it is still possible that the other might feel controlled — even though this was not your intent. Consider Vera's story. Vera has been dating Howie for six months. Howie has told her that he often felt overcontrolled as a child, and is therefore vigilant about others' attempts to control him. Through trial and error, Vera has discovered a good way to bring both herself and Howie more present. After stating a want, she checks in with Howie to find out how her request has come across.

Here's an example of how I have used Vera's discovery in my life. I call my partner at work to ask him to come home on time tonight so we can have a long, intimate evening together. While my aim is to be open and noncontrolling in my request, I can't help but recall times in the past when my partner has disclosed that my asking something like this resulted in his feeling controlled and choosing to stay at the office even later "just to assert my freedom." So now, as I consider making this request again, I feel some trepidation. In an effort to be transparent and vulnerable, I tell him, "I want you to come home on time tonight, and I also feel some fear about asking for this." Then I ask how he is feeling receiving my request — does it seem controlling? Does he feel resistance? Then I am silent as I listen to his response.

I Shouldn't Have to Ask

Many people inhibit asking for what they want because they believe "If he really loved me, he'd know what I like." They assume that the person should care enough and know them well enough to know what they want, without their having to ask for it. For people like this, asking is seen as equivalent to admitting to themselves that the other doesn't care very much. They think, "If I have to ask for it, it's less valuable" or "If he sincerely wanted to please me, he'd do it without my having to ask." Holding this attitude is another patterned way to avoid taking the risk of asking for what you want. When you operate as if this were true, you don't ask for very much, so you don't have to hear no very often. The problem is, by using this self-protection strategy, you miss the chance to develop the resilience and confidence that come from asking without knowing how the other person will respond. Obviously you can never know in advance how the other is going to receive your request — so asking is always a bit of a risk. But if the person cares about you, it is an intelligent risk. You will survive even if you hear a no, and either way, by opening yourself up to the unknown, you'll deepen your self-trust and begin to heal any outdated view you may have of yourself as too fragile.

> You will survive even if you hear a no, and either way, by opening yourself up to the unknown, you'll deepen your self-trust and begin to heal any outdated view you may have of yourself as too fragile.

I Don't Want to Feel Indebted

Yet another reason people give for not expressing wants is they assume that asking for something puts them in a one-down position. They may say, "Asking for attention or help puts me in a dependent relationship to the other person. I'm admitting that I can't do something. Feeling needy feels unattractive or uncomfortable" or "If I ask for and receive what I want, this means I'm beholden or indebted to the other."

If either of these sentiments is familiar to you, perhaps you harbor the unconscious belief that it's not okay or not safe to be needy or to depend on others. Where do you think this belief originated?

Most people who hold this belief have had a number of painful lessons early in life that gave them the idea that other people are not dependable. How supportive, competent, and reliable were your early caregivers? When or how did you learn that it's not safe to feel dependent or needy?

It may have been true in the past that some specific important person in your life was not dependable, but be careful about the mind's tendency to assume that the present will be a repeat of your past. The human ego-mind tries to protect you from harm by recording memories of danger and then alerting you whenever a similar danger may be present. But there is a problem in how the ego-mind operates: it tends to be overzealous in performing this self-protective function. It will tell you to avoid a situation if that situation appears even remotely similar to one that was painful in the past. This prevents you from learning two very important and real lessons: (1) that this present person is not the same person as the one who hurt you; and (2) even if the present situation does lead to pain or

> There is a problem in how the ego-mind operates: it tends to be overzealous in performing this self-protective function. It will tell you to avoid a situation if that situation appears even remotely similar to one that was painful in the past.

disappointment, you are bigger and more resourceful now, so you'll probably be able to cope. You will not be as devastated now (as an adult) when a loved one says, "I don't have time for you," as when you were a child. If you have trouble asking for help or attention, you may be stuck in a self-protective pattern stemming from a belief learned long ago. It's probably time to update your beliefs. Let the key phrase "I want..." be part of your self-healing program.

Types of Wants

There are several types of wants — asking for contact or attention; asking for space or the absence of contact; asking for tangible help (such as help with a project); and asking the other not to help you (as in, "I want you to listen and not try to fix it"). It is just as important to be able to say "I want space" (or absence of contact) as it is to say "I want time" (or contact). A very important in-the-moment request is "I don't want to respond to that right now." Often this will be in direct response to a partner's bid for information or attention. Give yourself permission to ask for more time, as in, "I'm not ready yet to answer that question or respond to that request. I need more time to check in with myself about that."

> Give yourself permission to ask for more time, as in, "I'm not ready yet to answer that question or respond to that request. I need more time to check in with myself about that."

Since it is common for a person who wants a lot of contact to pair up with a person who wants a lot of space, it's good to recognize that both types of wants are valid. The person who wants space needs to assert this just as forcefully as the person who wants contact. Otherwise the relationship will become lopsided — as if only one member of the pair, the one who likes more contact, has needs.

The Quid Pro Quo Response

In responding to requests, you can say *yes, no, maybe, not now,* or *I'll do that for you if you'll do this for me.*

It's important to give yourself permission to respond to someone's request with a request of your own (if this is a genuine need). For example, if your partner asks to talk about a recent disagreement, and you're reluctant to spend very much time on this, you might reply, "I hear what you want. And what I want is to get some sleep pretty soon. So I'll talk about it, if you'll agree to limit it to twenty minutes tonight." As this shows, sometimes your response is a conditional yes, or quid pro quo: "I'll give you what you want if you'll give me what I want." Some people don't like quid pro quos. They think these are too businesslike, too much like a negotiation; but there is a place for such exchanges in any mature relationship. Sometimes, if you're stretching yourself to fulfill a request, you need to take care of yourself by asking the other to stretch a little for you.

Blaming the Requester

Some people have a control pattern of getting indignant when a request is made of them, as in, "How could you ask that of me?" They'll criticize you for asking in order to avoid feeling the anxiety, fear, or internal pressure that your want creates. Perhaps they want to say no to your request, but they are afraid of your reaction, so they avoid feeling their fear by acting self-righteous.

Sandra and Dan's relationship exhibited this pattern. Whenever she would ask, "I'm wondering if you have any plans for this weekend," he would react, "Plans! Why do you always need to know my plans?! Why can't you just relax and go with the flow?" Dan could have just as easily responded with, "I haven't thought about that," or "I'm not into making plans for the weekend. I want to let things flow along." But he had an unconscious belief that "if a woman asks for plans, you have to give her plans!" In his story, you do not have the freedom to say, "I have no plans," or even "I don't want to talk about it now." We could speculate as to where this belief came from. It's likely that he is bringing an outdated assumption from his childhood into this present situation.

If you recognize yourself or someone you know in this example, take another look at what is actually being asked for, here and now. Ask yourself, What "surplus meaning" am I giving to the request, based on my past conditioning? Am I perhaps seeing the other's request as a demand or as a bid for control? Then notice that voice inside your own head that puts pressure on you — pressure that is coming from your own mind, not from the other person.

Allowing Yourself to Feel Disappointed

It's true that some people can't stand to disappoint anyone. The consequence of this fear of being a disappointment is that they're likely to feel controlled by almost any request. They do not give themselves permission to say no, but they project this lack of permission onto the other and imagine that she is being controlling and that it is not safe to say no to her.

> Some people can't stand to disappoint anyone. They're likely to feel controlled by almost any request.

If you are with someone who blames you when you make a request, how might you deliver your request in order to minimize this sort of misunderstanding? How can you get it across to him that you *can* take no for an answer, even as you ask for what you want? In my experience with this type of partner, I've found it helpful to state my want openly and simply and then to add, "And I want you to know that no is an okay answer." Then, if I ever do get a no, it's important to respond by sharing my feelings of disappointment, or whatever I feel, while at the same time appreciating him for being honest. Don't hide your disappointment if you feel it. Here's an example of saying what's real when I hear a no from this other person: "I'm really disappointed to hear that you don't want to spend the evening together, and at the same time, I so appreciate that you're saying how you really feel."

I believe that by letting my partner hear about my disappointment, I am helping him learn to tolerate the normal discomfort of "disappointing a woman." By not shielding him from my pain, I am helping him get used to feeling a type of discomfort that every healthy relationship needs to make room for. If he cannot allow me to feel unhappy with him sometimes, he's not a good prospect for a successful long-term relationship.

> If he cannot allow me to feel unhappy with him sometimes, he's not a good prospect for a successful long-term relationship.

You can help a partner like this heal from his past conditioning by showing him that you can handle hearing no and feeling disappointed without freaking out. And while you're at it, notice your own attitude about being disappointed. If you cannot handle hearing no, then you also are not a very good prospect for a successful long-term relationship. Two people are not always going to want the same thing at the same time. To create a healthy, mature relationship, both people need to feel free to refuse a request without fear of punishment. And they need to be willing to feel unhappy or disappointed with each other at times.

Do a Quick Self-Assessment

To assess your own level of maturity regarding wants, first examine your intent in asking for what you want. Does your "I want..." come from the intent to relate or to control? Remember, relating means expressing yourself in the interest of self-disclosure, not manipulation. Yes, you want what you want and make no apologies for this — even if you suspect your want is not reasonable. But you also want full self-expression for your partner and are interested in his or her genuine response to your request. Relating is two-way communication — coming from the desire to know and be known. When your intent is to relate, hearing a truthful response is more important to you than hearing yes.

Controlling is one-way. When your intent is to control, your energy and attention are focused on getting things to turn out the way you want or expect them to.

How Unreasonable Can a Want Be?

Pauline broke up with Fritz after dating him exclusively for a year. Her reason was that they were not as sexually compatible as she would have liked. Still, they really loved each other and had great times together. As they were ending things and attempting to redefine their relationship, she told him, "I'd like to date some other men, maybe for another year before I settle down and commit to someone. But if I don't meet anyone I like as well as I like you, I'll probably realize I made a mistake and want you back. I want you to wait for me."

To most people Pauline's request would seem unreasonable. How could she expect him to wait for her? Wasn't this awfully selfish? The truth is Fritz was perfectly free to say no, and Pauline did not say she *expected* him to wait. She simply asked for what she wanted.

Fritz's friends told him to forget her, she was just trying to use him. But he didn't forget her, even though he did date others during that year. In his heart he knew he was waiting to see if Pauline would come back to him. And after about a year, Fritz and Pauline did end up reconciling, much to onlookers' surprise.

The moral of this story is, go ahead and make any request you sincerely feel like making and let the other person decide for himself how to respond. Your request always contains important information about you. Pauline's request, for instance, contained some relevant information that Fritz needed in order to decide how to proceed. It's just as controlling to try to protect someone from knowing your true wants as it is to beat them over the head with your wants. A want is only a want. It is not a command or an order.

> It's just as controlling to try to protect someone from knowing your true wants as it is to beat them over the head with your wants. A want is only a want. It is not a command or an order.

How Asking for What You Want Helps You Heal

In this chapter I have mentioned a number of ways that this key phrase fosters emotional healing: it teaches you that *asking* is much more important than *getting* everything you ask for — thus teaching you to focus on what you can control (asking) instead of on what you cannot (whether you get it); it prompts you to speak about wants that you actually feel in the here and now, thus enhancing your capacity for present-centered contact; it prompts you to be specific about your wants, another way to enhance your personal presence; and it gives you permission to ask for anything and everything you desire rather than caretaking or protecting others from your wants. This helps you unhook from the notion that wants should be reasonable and that you need to protect others from your wants. Allowing yourself to want whatever you really want is an excellent way to affirm how innocent and noncontrolling the state of wanting really is. Wanting is making yourself vulnerable. It is not controlling.

> Allowing yourself to want whatever you really want is an excellent way to affirm how innocent and noncontrolling the state of wanting really is.

3 | I HAVE SOME FEELINGS TO CLEAR

There's something I've been withholding from you.
I have some anger to clear so we can get back to
feeling good with each other.
Can we talk about something that's been bothering me?
I have some feedback for you that could be hard to hear...
please know that my intent is not to hurt you but to make our
relationship better.

A ny way you say it, clearing the air needs to happen at some regular interval in all your significant relationships and on a daily basis if you want to be really intimate with a partner.

We have all experienced situations where two people relate harmoniously for a while, but then gradually, as more and more conflicts and disappointments are swept under the carpet, a wall begins to grow between them. Knowing how to clear the air using this key phrase helps to break down any wall that may be growing between you and your partner, and enables you to get back into present time with each other. If it's true that the most important prerequisite for good communication in a relationship is the ability to be present, then it's important to realize that when you are feeling incomplete about a recent or even a long-past incident, you can't be fully present. You're not "all there."

Many people resist bringing up old business for fear of making things worse or getting back into a frustrating discussion. If you have such concerns, it's not easy to take the steps necessary to overcome them because this would risk making a bigger mess. To get over the fear of conflict, you need to consciously take on the practice of having regular clearing sessions — sessions where you take turns expressing backed-up feelings. Besides helping you have more alive and real interactions, clearing the air regularly will teach you not to fear conflict, disagreement, or strong emotions. Using a regular clearing practice will give you confidence that such things can be faced and resolved.

> When you are feeling incomplete about a recent or even a long-past incident, you can't be fully present. You're not "all there."

Dealing Consciously with Conflict Avoidance

Jenny was one of those people who by her nature always hated conflict. But there came a point in her life where she realized that she had a pattern of choosing partners who seemed to thrive on anger, conflict, and strong emotions. So she had to ask herself, "Why do I keep choosing these people? I guess I'm not going to be able to get through life without developing better conflict skills."

At the time, she was partnered with a man who was easily provoked to anger, but who really didn't like conflict either. He simply had a lot of "buttons." They recognized that they both had a tendency to "stuff," or repress, their resentments. This was creating a wall of tension in their relationship.

They decided that if the relationship was to succeed, they would need to commit to a regular clearing practice. They began to set aside fifteen minutes every day to express their withheld irritations, disappointments, and anger. Both partners would take five- to eight-minute turns to share what the other had done or said, and what their feeling was, for example: "When you told me I looked like a clown, I felt hurt"; "When you didn't call to say you were going to be late, I felt angry." After each item, the listener would repeat back to the speaker what she had just said as a way to help her feel heard. Having your partner hear your anger helps you let go of your resentment — even if the situation doesn't change. And the practice of repeating back someone's beefs about you helps you realize that your partner's displeasure with you won't kill you. Eventually you'll become more open and present to whatever your partner is feeling.

> Clearing the air regularly will teach you not to fear conflict, disagreement, or strong emotions. Using a regular clearing practice will give you confidence that such things can be faced and resolved.

You'll learn to stay on your own side of the net and not take on the other's feelings as an indictment of you.

Sometimes when Jenny and her partner first started a clearing session, one or both of them couldn't think of anything that needed clearing, but if they dug a bit deeper and really searched, they could usually find something they had withheld. When doing this practice, they always made sure that both people had a turn to express their "withholds."

After expressing each resentment, they would check in with their feelings to see if they felt complete. If not, they'd try repeating their resentment until they felt more relaxed and connected. The goal of this exercise is to get back into harmony by speaking what you have been afraid to speak about.

Often, so much energy was released during these clearing sessions that they wound up laughing together. Jenny also reported that as she did this practice over the course of a year, she continued to feel more and more safe and comfortable in the presence of angry feelings. This helped her feel a deeper intimacy and safety in her relationship. She became less afraid of hearing, feeling, and expressing anger. She discovered that anger is just another feeling, and that if you can own your anger and express it responsibly, the energy formerly held in anger changes to aliveness.

She found that it really is possible to receive another's anger, and perhaps to feel hurt or scared by this, without shutting down your heart.

Jenny also learned not to be afraid of receiving her partner's anger. She found that it really is possible to receive another's anger, and perhaps to feel hurt or scared by this, without shutting down your heart.

Rituals Are Important

Many people do not realize they have been carrying a load of hurt or anger until someone invites them to do a clearing session. Then, "now that you mention it," they discover that they have quite a lot to clear as well. This is one reason it's good to "just do the practice" whether you think you need it or not. Most people in an intimate relationship will find feelings that need to be aired if they take the time to look.

Another good reason to just schedule a time for it is that most people are too busy

> Most people in an intimate relationship will find feelings that need to be aired if they take the time to look.

to fully feel and express difficult feelings at the time they occur. Our lives are often so full of tasks and projects that it doesn't occur to us to take a break to talk about upset feelings or unsatisfactory communications. This being the case, in both love and work relationships, partners need to commit to clearing the air at some regular, mutually agreed-upon interval.

HOW THESE RITUALS WORK

Once you have agreed that this is a good time to do your clearing ritual, begin with a statement like: "I have something to clear with you," "I have some withholds for you," or "Is there anything I have done recently that has created distance or resentment?" Take turns expressing your backed-up feelings. While your partner is speaking, ask her to pause frequently so you can repeat back what you have heard. This process of repeating what you have heard is called Active Listening. When she feels satisfied that you "got it," then it's your turn to express your backed-up feelings.

People who commit to using a regular clearing process report that their relationships stay juicy and alive. If you let resentments build up, more and more topics become taboo, unexpressed feelings create unconscious resentment, and the life goes out of your relationship.

There are a number of structures for clearing the air.

There are the feedback process, the resentments and appreciations process, and the withholds process.

In all these rituals, both people need to agree on the frequency and time limits for the sessions. In addition to your regularly scheduled time, these practices can also be done spontaneously anytime you need them. Don't think that just because you have a time set aside to share feedback in two days, you have to wait until then.

Designate a safe space for the ritual by choosing a place in your home or yard where you will be uninterrupted and where you can sit facing each other. It's helpful to do the ritual in the same place every time you do it. That way when you walk into this room or area, you have the sense that you are entering a different mind-set — a mind-set in which you set aside any need to prove your point or bolster your position. Your aim is transparency — to know and be known. We may fear that our resentments will appear selfish, petty, or unenlightened, so it may feel risky to reveal them. Remember that revealing resentments or withholds is an act of making yourself vulnerable.

> We may fear that our resentments will appear selfish, petty, or unenlightened, so it may feel risky to reveal them. Remember that revealing resentments or withholds is an act of making yourself vulnerable.

Some people like to sanctify the space by lighting a candle, smudging with sage, or burning incense.

Start each session by deciding who will go first. Try to take turns being the one who goes first. When it is the other person's turn, don't interrupt unless you need to ask him to be more specific. Then ask, "Can you be specific?" When you are finished, acknowledge your partner and yourself for the care and intention it takes to do such a practice.

Using Feedback to Clear the Air

The feedback ritual involves taking turns completing the sentence "When I heard you say... [or, "When I saw you do..."], I felt...." This is very similar to "Hearing you say that, I feel...," but in this case, you describe what the other specifically did or said, being careful to speak about *what actually happened* and not *your inferences or interpretations* about the other's motives or intent. For example, "When you walked out in the middle of my sharing, I felt anger." You would not say, "When you were rude to me, I felt anger." "You were rude" is an interpretation. It is also good to add a statement about where in your body you experienced this: "When you walked out in the middle of my sharing, I felt the heat of anger rising in my face." This brings your attention into your body.

Here's an example of how one couple used feedback to clear the air. Frank and Luanne had recently gone to a large party at a country estate. During the course of the four-hour evening, there was a period of over two hours where Luanne didn't see Frank and could not find him anywhere in the house. There were several rooms where the party was taking place, and although she looked everywhere for him, he seemed to have disappeared. Then, at around twelve-thirty he walked in from the backyard, laughing and talking with one of her women friends. When she gave him feedback about this on the drive home, here's what she said: "When I was looking around for you in all the rooms at the party, I felt disappointed and hurt. When I saw you walking in the house with Ginny, I felt a bit relieved, but I was still left with the idea that you would rather be with someone else than with me. When I think this thought, I feel a pain in my belly."

If Luanne had said nothing to Frank, her disappointment might have dissipated in time, but when something like this is not cleared, it is stored in the unconscious part of the mind, waiting until the next time Frank does something similar. Then he's likely to hear about her pent-up feelings. The advantage of doing this feedback ritual consciously is it keeps you up-to-date with each other.

> If partners clear the air regularly, they aren't as likely to be blind-sided by a list of things they've done wrong during the entire history of the relationship.

If partners clear the air regularly, they aren't as likely to be blindsided by a list of things they've done wrong during the entire history of the relationship. If you have ever been on the receiving end of such a barrage of past grievances, you know that this erodes trust and can be quite hurtful.

RECEIVING FEEDBACK

When you are receiving feedback, pause and take it in. Notice the sensations and feelings in your body. Do you feel relaxed or contracted, open or defended? Notice your thoughts: Do you agree with the feedback or not? Do you feel any internal pressure to change yourself or your behavior? Remember: it is your choice what you do about the feedback. You are not obligated to change anything. Listen to your self-talk.

Did your inner critic get triggered? Did you automatically discount what was said? Did you get defensive and start explaining?

In replying to feedback, keep it simple. After you have taken some time to really take in what the other has told you, acknowledge her for what she has said. If the feedback is surprising or troubling, acknowledge this without agreeing or disagreeing with the content — at least at this point. It's also a good idea to practice Active Listening if the feedback is hard to hear. Repeating what you have just heard keeps you centered, so you're less likely to overreact. It gives you time to assimilate the feedback before responding.

> When you are receiving feedback, pause and take it in. Notice the sensations and feelings in your body. Do you feel relaxed or contracted, open or defended?

If the feedback is vague or general, or if you're not clear what the other person means, ask her to be more specific. This is important. Asking for specifics is different from being defensive. If you're going to learn anything, and if the other person is going to clear the air successfully, both of you need to know what you specifically did and what she felt.

In receiving feedback, see if you can adopt an attitude of openness to learning. Avoid making excuses or blaming. I have seen so many relationships destroyed when they could have been healed simply because the person receiving feedback could not handle the feelings that were triggered by it and went immediately into a defensive or aggressive control pattern.

It is good practice when you're first using the feedback

ritual to receive it without much verbal response, breathing slowly and deeply. This helps you learn to fully experience the other's words and your feelings. Being quiet and noticing your breath is especially important if you tend to get triggered easily. Sometimes a quick comeback is an escape from feeling the discomfort of your true feelings. If you're uncomfortable, it's good to be aware of this. Embrace your discomfort consciously.

When people see you as able to receive feedback and to be with your feelings instead of controlling the situation to avoid discomfort, they feel well-received, and they tend to trust you more. They feel safer about saying what's real and sharing things they might otherwise withhold. And they get over what was bothering them. If you do choose to verbally respond to the feedback right away, start by sharing your experience as you hear the feedback: What sensations are you aware of in your body? What emotions do you feel? What thoughts, judgments, and self-talk come up? These are what you need to share. "Hearing you say that about me, I feel relieved. I was afraid you were going to say that it's over between us." Or, "Hearing you say this, I feel some defensiveness. My self-talk is, 'Should I explain myself or just take in what you are saying?'"

Listening to feedback is different from agreeing with it or taking it on as your responsibility to do something about.

Being open to feedback does not mean you automatically accept the other's impressions of you as the truth. It means letting the feedback in and letting it have an impact on you. Listening to feedback is different from agreeing with it or taking it on as your responsibility to do something about. You weigh it in light of other things you have seen in yourself and in the person delivering the feedback and in light of other people's feedback on the same issue. You are the one who decides whether or not to make changes based on what you have heard.

The Resentments and Appreciations Ritual

In this ritual, each person takes a turn completing the sentence "I resent you for saying/doing..." (something specific that the other did, said, or did not do).

After you have both shared your resentments, then take turns telling each other some specific things that you appreciate, using the form "I appreciate you for..." (something specific). Be generous with your appreciations. As you start appreciating more, you will strengthen your ability to appreciate, and you'll find yourself discovering more and more things to appreciate. You will become more sensitive to feelings of appreciation.

Before the close of the ritual, share something that you appreciate about yourself. End it by appreciating each other for engaging in the practice.

I recommend the exact words "I appreciate you for..." for several reasons. First, saying "I" helps keep you grounded in your own experience. Second, using an "I...you" sentence helps you feel the connection between you and the other person. It helps you learn to feel comfortable making strong statements, and it helps you learn not to lose yourself in the face of powerful contact. The ability to make strong contact is a prerequisite for intimacy. Third, stating what the other specifically did or didn't do helps create a felt sense in your body. Being in your body as you speak helps you move through your feelings so you can get to forgiveness, if appropriate. Being specific also eliminates the temptation to argue over conflicting interpretations. It keeps you focused on an actual memory of what happened rather than on an interpretation. Being specific is harder for some people than for others, but it will get easier as you do the practice. Even if you can only partially recall the specifics, they are still helpful. Don't get perfectionistic about it.

If, after trying, you can't be specific, then use a phrase like, "I resent you for what I interpret (or imagine) as your inability to hear my anger." Of course, it's better to say: "I resent you for not looking at me and for turning away from me when I expressed my anger." But sometimes the specifics escape us.

Sometimes when you cannot find specific words to express a resentment, it's okay to talk about what was *not* done, as in: "I resent you for not telling me you were going out in the yard with Ginny." This signals that I had an expectation that was disappointed, and I'm taking responsibility for it.

RECEIVING RESENTMENTS

When receiving resentments, see if you can be spacious enough to allow the other to have feelings, even if hearing them causes you pain or upset. Just notice your upset and the thoughts and feelings associated with it.

If you are receiving a resentment, and your partner is

making an inference or interpretation without telling you the behavior or data this is based on, ask, "Can you be specific?" This is a signal for the partner to recognize that she or he is making an assumption or an interpretation. It also gives you time to get centered so you'll be less likely to overreact.

Don't expect your partner to offer specific details of *everything* you may have done or said to trigger the resentment. If your partner can only remember part of what you said or did, try not to let your "I'm being misunderstood" button get pushed. Even if he can only recall a fragment of what you said, this can still help him clear the air.

RESENTMENT DOES NOT EQUAL BLAME

Some people think that sharing resentments using the words "I resent you for..." implies that you're blaming the other. This is not the case. The "I resent you for..." sentence structure does not imply that the other is responsible for your feelings. Expressing your resentment does not imply that the other did something wrong or that she caused your reaction. Likewise, you can feel resentment without thinking that you are right. Feelings are not right or wrong. They do not need to appear reasonable or justifiable. I use this structure for sharing feelings to help people have the experience of expressing themselves strongly and discovering how well this works to clear the air. This ritual is especially recommended for people who shy

> Expressing your resentment does not imply that the other did something wrong or that she caused your reaction. Likewise, you can feel resentment without thinking that you are right. Feelings are not right or wrong.

> Once you clear the anger out of the way, it's easier to feel the love.

away from strong contact. The lesson these folks need to learn is that someone can feel anger toward you and love you at the same time. Once you clear the anger out of the way, it's easier to feel the love.

The Withholds Ritual

Sharing withholds is another useful practice for clearing the air and overcoming your fears about conflict. It's a bit more controlled, so for most people it's less scary than sharing resentments. I learned this process back in 1974 at More University in Lafayette, California. Partner A starts: "John, there's something I've withheld from you." Partner B says, "Okay, would you like to tell me?" Then, Partner A relates something she felt or thought, such as, "I felt disappointed that you did not get me a birthday present." Partner B says, "Thank you." The "thank you" signals the end of that turn. If Partner B feels a need to bring up the issue again, he can do so during his turn, as in, "Jane, there's something I've withheld from you." Partner A says, "Okay," and then Partner B might say, "I feel sorry that I didn't at least make you a card. If I could do it over, I'd plan way ahead and get you something really special." Then Partner A says, "Thank you."

Saying "thank you" is an important part of the practice, because it acknowledges the other person for being candid. It does not necessarily mean the speaker is pleased. It keeps the partners from getting into a discussion, since the purpose of sharing withholds is simply to share information about your current reality. Often doing so is all that is needed to resolve the issue.

Resentments or appreciations could also be expressed within the structure of sharing withholds. So could feedback in the form of "When I heard you say/when you did..., I felt..." (as described above). Here's how one couple used the feedback form in sharing withholds:

KELLY: There's something I've withheld from you.

HOWIE: Okay, would you like to tell me?

KELLY: Yes, when you left the door to the garage open all night, I felt angry.

HOWIE: Thank you.

Sometimes, especially if the content of the withhold is likely to trigger a reaction, it's good to use Active Listening in conjunction with sharing withholds. In this process, one person is the talker and the other is listener. When it is Partner A's turn, he states his feelings or views. Partner B listens and then says what she heard A say, reflecting back both content and feelings. Active Listening is a wonderful tool to use when two people are having a conflict or disagreement. It helps you stay focused on what you are hearing when it might be difficult to stay present and really listen — like when you don't agree with what's being said.

If you ever notice your partner getting defensive while listening to your feedback, this is another good time to employ Active Listening. After hearing his comments, repeat back to him what you heard (both the content and the feelings). Doing this gives you a way to stay centered and nonreactive — so you don't meet his defensiveness with more defensiveness. It gives your mind something to do. Then you can hear him with more spaciousness in your awareness. So, instead of saying, "Stop getting defensive," you'd say what you just heard: "I hear that you don't remember saying you'd get me the money by Friday."

Using a Preamble to Create Safety

If I'm expressing anger to someone who has a pattern of avoiding conflict, getting reactive, or taking my anger personally, I like to begin my invitation to clear the air with a preamble that reassures him that my anger is not a permanent condition. I'll get over it if I have the chance to express it. So, even if we're doing one of the above-mentioned clearing rituals (and especially if I'm bringing this up out of the blue), I'll start by saying, "I have some anger to clear with you, and I want you to remember that I'll probably be over it once I've talked about it." That simple introduction can make a huge difference in the other person's ability to receive my anger. The statement also firms up my own intent to express the anger consciously rather than punitively and then let it go.

Developing Spaciousness of Attention

These clearing rituals help you continually clear away old unfinished business so you can be present to what is actually going on here and now. They help you develop a more spacious, less reactive consciousness.

They are actually "awareness practices" as well as tools for keeping your relationship up-to-date. They free you from the need to control how others view you by helping you get over feeling responsible for their feelings. They teach you that you can listen to viewpoints that differ from yours without losing touch with your own viewpoint.

Another important lesson that comes from practicing these rituals is the fact that once you express a feeling, it often changes, whereas when you don't express feelings, they stick around in your subconscious and become magnified. It's important to learn that feelings come and go and need not be all that scary or significant. At the same time, they deserve to be felt, expressed, and cleared.

> These clearing rituals help you continually clear away old unfinished business so you can be present to what is actually going on. They help you develop a more spacious, less reactive consciousness.

All these clearing rituals are designed to be short and sweet. You simply say what you experienced (what you saw or heard and what you felt or thought), being very specific. You are not asking the other to change anything. If you find that you need to resolve a conflict or go deeper into understanding each other's viewpoint, then spend some additional time interviewing each other and practicing Active Listening.

Clearing the Air at Work

Whenever I'm coaching people in the workplace who want to be politically successful in the company, I always encourage them to set up regular clearing sessions with their superiors, peers, and employees. Clearing the air regularly means that people won't be gossiping about you or backstabbing you, because they've gotten a chance to air their grievances face to face and therefore have probably gotten over them. But more important, by receiving feedback frequently, you are continually learning and improving your performance, a vital ingredient in a successful career.

After being promoted to manager, Todd decided to have monthly clearing sessions with his supervisor and everyone who reported to him. His goal was to make sure he got the information he needed to serve his internal customers. But as time went on, he observed another benefit to this as well: his teammates seemed to feel more relaxed around him and were more apt to approach him with problems before these problems became crises. Before the regular check-in sessions began, they had not been so forthcoming.

> Clearing the air regularly means that people won't be gossiping about you or backstabbing you, because they've gotten a chance to air their grievances face to face.

Clearing Anger with a Parent

Almost everyone has unfinished business with one or both parents, whether the parent is dead or alive. If you do not express and clear this old baggage, not only will your relationship with your parents be compromised, but so will your other significant relationships. Remember, a clearing ritual can be used with anyone you're close to or would like to feel closer to. Although the prospect of clearing with a parent is often uncomfortable, people who have done this report that after even one such clearing session, what had been a lifeless or strained relationship comes alive again.

Here's how you might begin: "Mom, I'd like for us to make a time when we can sit down together and talk about the things that happened between us when I was living at home with you and Dad. Are you open to doing this?" Then wait for as long as it takes for her to respond, and when she does, really listen. If she does not give a clear

> People who have done this report that after even one such clearing session, what had been a lifeless or strained relationship comes alive again.

yes or no, say "Is that a yes?" (Or "Is that a no?") Then tell her that your intent is to talk about anything that was done or said that left either of you with feelings of anger, mistrust, guilt, hurt, shame, or sadness. Tell her that the purpose is to get free of these troublesome feelings from the past by getting them out in the open. The idea is not to blame or accuse, and not to explain, defend, or fix anything that happened, but rather to acknowledge the things that did happen and to express feelings about them. Mention that just doing this leads to healing because facing and accepting our feelings, bringing light to things formerly hidden, allows us to integrate old hurts and traumas and bring them into relationship with our more conscious and healthy aspects. Now instead of having certain unacceptable things split off from the whole of ourselves, we bring these split-off parts into their appropriate relationship with our stronger and more valued parts.

Once you have agreed to do a clearing session, decide together on a good time to have the conversation. Face-to-face is best. And be sure both people get an uninterrupted turn to express what they remember experiencing. Once you have both had your turn, check in to see if you feel lighter and more open. If not, go back over anything that feels incomplete. Explain to your parent that sometimes it's necessary to repeat yourself in order to get fully into a feeling so you can get to completion and forgiveness. After you express a strong feeling, notice what you feel now to see if that feeling has changed or disappeared. If the feeling changes or feels resolved, let it go. If it persists, express it again until you feel a noticeable degree of relaxation or relief.

Practicing with Friends

If you are not in a relationship where it is appropriate to set aside a regular time for clearing, I have created three fun, interactive card games that you can use with friends, acquaintances, or workmates: the Getting Real Card Game for general audiences, the Truth at Work Card Game for work teams, and the Truth in Dating Card Game for couples, groups, and new relationships. These games ask players to answer self-revealing questions such as "What has the other person done or said recently that created distance between you?" and "What is something you have thought about the person across from you but have not told him/her?" The games also offer the option of asking for feedback after your answers, so people do not leave with unfinished business. All three games are customizable to fit the comfort level of your particular group. Ordering information about these games is available in Appendix A.

Why Clear the Air?

The main benefit of all these clearing practices is they keep your mind free to focus on what is here and now between yourself and another person. When you are present to this moment, you are more creative, resourceful, and realistic. You see more clearly what is really happening instead of allowing your childhood beliefs and fears (in the form of mind chatter) to run the show.

CHAPTER

4 I'M GETTING TRIGGERED

What you just said is triggering a reaction.
I notice I'm having a reaction.
I'm starting to get defensive.
I think I'm getting a button pushed.
I'm getting my "not good enough" button pushed.
I'm getting triggered.

Rhonda couldn't stand it when her boyfriend Stan spent time at his buddy Roger's place. She knew that Roger's attractive younger sister had a crush on Stan, so whenever he came home from Roger's house, she would interrogate him thoroughly — making sure to find out exactly how long he had spent in the sister's company.

Leo hated how his supervisor Monique seemed to speak to everyone but him in a warm tone of voice. When she spoke with him, it seemed that Monique always had a critical edge to her voice. He always felt small around her.

Keith got uncomfortable when his mother asked him to do favors for her, particularly if it was something he didn't want to do. But instead of saying no or telling her "Not now," Keith would respond by accusing her of being too demanding.

These three scenarios are examples of how people behave when one of their unconscious fears gets triggered. Often, if someone's present circumstance reminds him of a frightening or painful situation in his past, this will cause a knee-jerk negative reaction.

When you find yourself overreacting like this, it means that one of your old fears has been triggered, such as the fear that you're not loveable or the fear of being controlled. When this happens, I recommend using the key phrase "I'm getting triggered." This brings more awareness to the interaction. It helps you step back and notice yourself behaving in an automatic way.

> If someone's present circumstance reminds him of a frightening or painful situation in his past, this will cause a knee-jerk negative reaction.

The reactions of Rhonda, Leo, and Keith were out of proportion to the situations they found themselves in. This makes it hard for others to empathize with them. Being triggered like this also creates confusion and stress, so they are unable to perceive their full range of options. Using the phrase "I'm getting triggered" helps you see yourself more objectively. It communicates to others that you are at least somewhat present and aware.

Noticing and revealing your reaction can also foster self-acceptance. It's like saying to yourself, "It's okay that I just got triggered. This is part of being a human being with human emotions. Now let's get back to the here and now."

When you use some version of this key phrase, you are bringing yourself present as opposed to staying stuck in an unconscious reaction. Once you learn to accept that you sometimes do get defensive or reactive, your tendency to overreact will probably diminish simply as a function of becoming a more conscious human being.

> Once you learn to accept that you sometimes do get defensive or reactive, your tendency to overreact will probably diminish simply as a function of becoming a more conscious human being.

Using This Key Phrase in Marriage

Joseph had a gut-tightening reaction whenever his wife, Janice, came to him to express hurt or upset feelings — even if these feelings had nothing to do with him. After noticing this for a while, he began to wonder: "Why do I always want to get away when she shares her upsets with me? Why can't I just listen without feeling so panicky?" The answer to his question came after much counseling and soul-searching. When he was a youngster, his mom, a single parent, had frequently used him as a sounding board for her personal problems. At the time, he had felt too small to hold all of his mom's feelings but too powerless to protest. The truth was he never felt comfortable listening to his mom's problems. It seemed that Janice was doing the same thing — except now, it should have been okay. As her mate, it would ordinarily be appropriate for him to be her "shoulder to cry on." And while Joseph saw that he was stuck in an old pattern of resisting being leaned on, he could not change his reaction.

With the help of some relationship coaching, the pair got a fresh perspective on the vicious cycle they were in. As fate would have it, their patterns were at odds. Whenever Joseph shut down while she was expressing feelings, Janice got triggered. She had come from a large family where she typically had trouble getting anyone to listen to her needs and frustrations. From that early experience she developed the fear that "no one wants to listen to me... my feelings are a burden to others."

Working with their coach, the pair began to recognize that any time Janice had feelings to share, she would go into an anxiety reaction, her throat getting tight and her voice shaky. She would have this reaction even before she opened her mouth! So, of course, whenever she expressed herself, she wasn't really present. Joseph would feel a growing sense of dread as he sensed her stifled emotions. If we couple her obvious tension with the fact that he already had resistance to being a woman's sounding board, we have here a recipe for mutual frustration. When two people are triggered at the same time, it can be extremely upsetting for both parties.

> "I notice I'm having a reaction to what you're saying" signals to the other partner a level of self-awareness that tends to help him feel safer.

What can a couple do when they find themselves both overreacting at once, repeating the same fight over and over and never getting anywhere? An important first step is for at least one of the pair to get fluent with the language, "I notice I'm having a reaction to what you're saying." This signals to the other partner a level of self-awareness that tends to help him feel safer.

He hears his partner's sensitivity, and that she is taking responsibility for her reaction rather than blaming him.

Using this key phrase helps partners get beyond blame. Blaming is a control pattern. It's a way to feel more in control by explaining why something occurred — when in fact, you do not know why. You feel helpless, and finding something or someone to blame helps you feel less helpless. ("I'm feeling bad because of you. If you hadn't done that, I wouldn't be feeling bad.") Blaming supports the illusion that you have identified the cause of your suffering.

> Blaming is a control pattern. It's a way to feel more in control by explaining why something occurred. You feel helpless, and finding something or someone to blame helps you feel less helpless.

In the case of Joseph and Janice, even if only one of them masters this all-important statement, that's a good start. How does a couple proceed after one of them admits to being in reaction? If it is Joseph who says, "I'm triggered," where does this leave Janice? In my experience, if Janice hears this admission from Joseph, it helps her feel safer because he is not blaming her for his reaction. He is owning it as *his* trigger. It may also help her become more conscious of her own feeling state and more aware that she too is caught in a reaction. So Janice can use this as her cue to admit, "I'm triggered, as well." Now both of them are more present to their own feelings rather than holding the position that "he (or she) ought to stop pushing my buttons!"

To help Joseph and Janice learn to step back and notice their reactions, I taught them to be more aware of their bodily sensations — to notice when they were relaxed and when they felt tense. After working with the pair for a few sessions, I was delighted to see them using this phrase whenever they noticed their bodies tightening up in fear. One evening during a session, Janice shared with Joseph her frustrations about being a new mom. Instead of his usual pattern of withdrawing, Joseph was able to fully experience the numbing and tightening going on in his chest — a signal that he was being triggered. He reported, "I can feel my body getting tense; I think I'm getting my button pushed — my button about being unloaded on by my mother. This feeling in my body feels very familiar. It's the way I felt when I was about eleven, and Mom was dating two different men and asking me about which one to marry. I wanted to say, 'Don't ask me. I'm just a little kid!' But I just sat there and listened and got more and more numb."

As Joseph heard himself and noticed the emotions welling up in him, he came to accept his extreme sensitivity to being leaned on by a woman. With acceptance came a lessening of the intensity of his reaction. The button didn't go away completely, but now, whenever he feels this reaction coming on, he knows how to soothe himself for the pain he suffered in the past and then bring himself back to the present time.

Facing Someone's Anger

Most people get triggered when someone directs anger at them — particularly if the anger comes without warning.

Darol took Marie by surprise when he scolded, "How many times have I asked you to save your receipts?" Marie's normal reaction would be to defend herself, as in, "I'm doing the best I can. Can't you see how overwhelmed I am dealing with these kids and a family business?" Defensive reactions like this are normal in most relationships — but they do not build intimacy. Defensiveness erodes trust and loving feelings.

If Marie knew how to talk openly about her triggers, she might be able to tell Darol that his anger scares her — thus her defensive reaction. If she would tell him, "I'm triggered by what you said, and I'm feeling defensive," this would put her firmly in touch with herself.

> When you are present to yourself, you naturally feel stronger — because you are giving yourself permission to be as you are, rather than denying or masking your true feelings.

When you are present to yourself, you naturally feel stronger — because you are giving yourself permission to be as you are, rather than denying or masking your true feelings. By expressing yourself responsibly and authentically, you are creating a powerful self-affirmation. Avoiding and hiding from painful feelings weakens your connection to yourself. Acknowledging what you feel builds confidence and self-trust, which will make it easier for you to face difficult situations in the future.

In the Midst of an Argument

If two people are stuck in an argument, both people's buttons are probably being pushed at the same time. When this is going on, how can partners extricate themselves? It's not as hard as it may seem. The secret is this: if just one of the pair will admit, "I'm being triggered here. I'm reacting. I'm on automatic," this brings the whole conversation to a higher level of truth and transparency. When one person becomes humble and aware enough to make this key statement, it is like a wake-up call, inviting both people into the present moment. We recognize how un-present we are, and paradoxically, this brings us present.

> If just one of the pair will admit, "I'm being triggered here. I'm reacting. I'm on automatic," this brings the whole conversation to a higher level of truth and transparency. We recognize how un-present we are, and paradoxically, this brings us present.

It's Hard to Hear No

Something that pushes most people's buttons is being refused when they ask for what they want. Disappointment is a real button-pusher. If you are someone who has an especially difficult time hearing no, it's good to be aware of it. This will help you be more ready to notice your reaction when someone refuses your request.

What is the fear associated with this reaction? In my case, I have a sensitivity about being refused when I ask someone for intimate touch. When I was an infant, my mom was shy about her body and didn't like too much physical touching. So she pushed me away from her many times when I would approach her for hugs and physical nurturance. As a result I took on a negative belief or fear that I'm not okay or not good enough. Since becoming aware of this childhood fear, I have learned that when I have this reaction, it helps bring me present if I can name the reaction as in, "I'm getting my 'I'm not good enough' fear reactivated." This gives my partner a little more information than if I simply said, "I'm having a reaction"; and it helps him feel that I'm taking responsibility for my reaction (vs. blaming him), so he's more likely to feel compassion toward me.

Being Interrupted Mid-sentence

Everyone has had the experience of being interrupted. If this is a sensitive area for you, and you are aware of it, you'll be better prepared to stay present when interruptions happen to you. What's the fear about? Are you afraid you're not interesting to others? Not significant? Not valued or valuable? The better you are at naming the fear associated with the button, the easier it will be for the other person to hear you and feel compassionate toward you — and the more compassionate you will feel toward yourself.

> The better you are at naming the fear associated with the button, the easier it will be for the other person to hear you and feel compassionate toward you — and the more compassionate you will feel toward yourself.

If someone close to you interrupts you often, get good at using this key phrase. You might say something like:

- "When you started talking over my words, I got triggered. I think it's my fear that I'm not important."

- "When you began your answer before I was finished asking my question, I had a reaction. I imagined you didn't care about me. That's my fear that I'm not loveable."

- "When you spoke before I was finished, I got my 'I'm not worth listening to' button pushed."

KNOW YOUR BUTTONS

If you can name your buttons, they are less likely to have power over you. The best insurance against having your fears control your life is knowing what they are. To help you identify your buttons, here is a paper-and-pencil activity you can do to assess your fears.

Make a copy of the following questionnaire for your partner. Each of you should write your answers privately and then discuss them.

1. Think of instances in your past relationships when your buttons have been pushed and you have been reactive or defensive in response. On a sheet of paper, list several specific examples following the format below:

    Button-pushing event:_____
    Fear that got triggered:_____

On the first line, list a specific thing that a prior partner did that triggered you. Then, below each item you listed, name the fear that got triggered. To illustrate how this might look, here's how one of my workshop participants, Roy, responded:

A. Button-pushing event: *Shirley said, "Let me handle it."*
   Fear that got triggered: *I'm stupid.*
B. Button-pushing event: *Shirley said, "Isn't that rice overdone?"*
   Fear that got triggered: *I'm incompetent.*
C. Event: *Doris said, "Don't ever do that again!"*
   Fear: *I'm a disappointment.*
D. Event: *Doris said, "You don't get me, and you never will."*
   Fear: *I'm incompetent and I'm a disappointment.*
E. Event: *Molly said, "When are you going to fix that door?"*
   Fear: *I'm not capable.*

2. Next, write down what hurtful, scary, or disappointing event(s) from your childhood may have instilled the fear or belief you listed in each scenario above.

Here is how Roy described the origins of his *I'm not capable* fear mentioned in scenario E:

When I was five, my dad was showing me how to help him put together a plastic playhouse he had just bought for me.

I was struggling to get two of the parts to fit together, and all of a sudden, he grabbed them away from me and said something like, "Here, I can do it faster. Just let me do it." I felt extremely small and ashamed when he did that. I thought he was saying I was too stupid, too inept to do it myself.

3. How did you overreact in each of the triggering events you listed above?

Here is Roy's response for scenario E:

When Molly said, "When are you going to fix that door?" I said, "Well, I was going to fix it today, but now you've made me so mad I think I need to wait till next weekend. You know I can't stand it when you push me like that."

4. Next, complete the following sentence for each of the instances you listed:

If, at the time, I had felt safe enough or been aware enough to express my true feelings, here's what I would have said: _____.

Here is how Roy responded:

A. *Hearing you say, "Let me handle it," I feel irritated. I also feel small and ashamed.*

B. *I imagine you're trying to tell me something with that question. I want you to say what you are feeling instead of asking me, "Isn't that rice overdone?"*

C. *When you say that to me, I feel a knot in my gut.*

D. *When you say that I don't get you, I feel sad. I'm thinking to myself that I must be a disappointment to you.*

E. *I get angry when you ask me when I'm going to fix the door. I get my "I'm being controlled" button pushed. This triggers my fear that you don't think I can handle things and that you think I'm not competent.*

5. In what ways have you done something to spite another person or get back at them for pushing one of your buttons? List three examples.

Here's one of Roy's examples:

When I was married to Lois, she was talking one day about how great her dad was. I thought she was implying that I could never match that, so I started telling her how well my former lover Bonnie had taken care of me, how nurturing and attentive she had been. This was right after Lois had given birth to our second child. She wasn't giving me much attention, and I was pissed. And I was also pissed at her remark about her dad.

> The ideal partner is not someone who never has unconscious reactions. It's someone who can take responsibility for her own reactions without blaming you.

When Roy and his partner Ruth shared their answers to this questionnaire, they got to see some of the ways they had reacted unconsciously in the past. This helped them be more aware and accepting of one another's triggers. The ideal partner is not someone who never has unconscious reactions. It's someone who can take responsibility for her own reactions without blaming you.

Benefits of Using This Key Phrase

Learning to get fluent with the phrase "I'm getting triggered" has several benefits: It helps you get over the belief that you'd feel better if only your partner would change — because it helps you take responsibility for your own reactions. It helps your partner feel safer and more open to hearing you. And it brings you into the present moment. Being in the present gives you more confidence and resourcefulness to deal with what is actually going on now. It helps you see that your current reaction is based more on fear than on reality.

5

I APPRECIATE YOU FOR...

I appreciate you for telling me what you want.
I appreciate you for doing the dishes last night.
I appreciate you for the way you're looking at me right now.
I appreciate you for getting your term project
done a week before the deadline.
I appreciate you for saying you'll get into treatment
for your alcoholism.

When I do coaching with couples and families, I often end the session by asking everyone to share a few specific appreciations with one another — stating in concrete terms something each person did or said that created a feeling of warmth, appreciation, or closeness. Often when people do this, they realize how nourishing it is, how good it feels to hear how they have impacted those they love in a positive way. Frequently, as they leave the session, they have tears in their eyes.

"Why don't we ever do this at home?" they ask. Good question. I think "appreciations" is a foreign language for many of us. In our families of origin, it was not done regularly, so the habit has not been established.

I include this statement as one of the seven most vital to

relationship success because it brings pleasure and healing to people. This is a bonding experience. A strong relationship bond makes it possible for couples and families (and friends and co-workers, too!) to weather the inevitable rough spots in a relationship. Sharing appreciations on a regular basis is an investment in the health of your relationship. It's like feeding your relationship vitamins so it will be more resilient under stress.

> A strong relationship bond makes it possible for couples and families (and friends and co-workers, too!) to weather the inevitable rough spots in a relationship.

Ashley and Scott had been married only a year when Scott found out that Ashley was having a secret affair with one of his buddies. They sought counseling to help them decide if the marriage was salvageable. During their sessions with me, they discovered that the main issue for Ashley was that she longed to hear words of love and appreciation from Scott; but because of his rather aloof personality style, he avoided this sort of expression. They had argued about this during their first year of marriage, but Ashley had soon concluded that she would have to go elsewhere for emotional strokes. When Scott discovered that she had found what she was looking for in another man, he was devastated.

After a few counseling sessions, he decided that he wanted to learn to be more expressive about his appreciations, even though this did not come naturally for him. Being raised in a family where tender feelings were not expressed, Scott had adopted the belief that anyone who needs verbal reassurance is somehow weak or inferior. After learning to empathize with his wife's feelings through our counseling, he revised this belief.

At first, he had to spend time alone before each session making a list of the specific things about Ashley that he appreciated. Since he wasn't skilled at thinking on his feet about such things, it worked best for him to sit down every day and write one or two things Ashley had done that day that he appreciated. I asked him to be sure that his list included qualities as well as behaviors — qualities such as how her body looked and how much he enjoyed her sense of humor.

At first, Ashley had difficulty trusting Scott's sincerity when he expressed his appreciations. She could hear the tentativeness in his voice. But such tentativeness is to be expected from someone who is learning a new language. Tenderness was not his native tongue. He had been taught the language of tough-mindedness, not the language of the heart. She also had trouble letting go of her fear, "Why now, all of a sudden, now that I'm pulling away...why does he only now appreciate me?" These doubts are understandable. But the fact is, people usually speak their appreciations awkwardly, self-consciously, and therefore tentatively, when they are first learning. And it's also a common occurrence that some people need a crisis to wake them up and make them pay attention to something that was there all along — in this case Scott's love, appreciation, and devotion to Ashley. She had not felt it before, but it had always been there.

> Tentativeness is to be expected from someone who is learning a new language. Tenderness was not his native tongue. He had been taught the language of tough-mindedness, not the language of the heart.

In every weekly session, Scott and Ashley practiced

telling each other specific things they had appreciated about each other during the previous week. A coach is often needed to help partners learn to pay attention to specifics. Being specific was hard even for Ashley. If one of them offered a generalization, such as, "I appreciate you for being so nice to me after we made love," I would intervene and ask, "What did she do that you call nice?" The reasons for being specific are: (1) you'll both know what the specific behavior is that's being discussed, which reinforces the probability that the behavior will be repeated; and (2) you're more in your body, and therefore more present, when you are actually recalling a specific behavior in your mind's eye.

Appreciation Brings You into the Present

As we have seen repeatedly, anything that brings you and another into the present moment together expands your capacity for intimacy and trust. Being present to your feelings while being consciously aware of your connection to each other doesn't just improve your most intimate relationships. It also deepens your capacity for connection with others in your life.

Telling someone specifically what he did that you appreciate brings more presence to the interaction in two ways: (1) you are sharing a present-time feeling; and (2) you are describing what was specifically done or said in a way that brings the memory back to life, and thus into present time.

I like to use this key phrase to bring me back into my heart and my body any time I find myself indulging worries and fears about the future of a relationship. When I'm feeling insecure or uncertain, I have a tendency to focus on my fears, giving attention to something that will probably never happen instead of staying with what is actually going on now. I have found that expressing appreciations interrupts such mind chatter, bringing me back to something more real and present.

Most fears are fantasies about something that could happen in the future. Being present is inherently empowering. Your attention is focused where it ought to be — on the things you can affect. Being on a head-trip about things that may or may not ever happen is disempowering; your attention is on things you cannot affect.

The most important thing about being in present time is this: when you're present, fear is absent. I think this is because most fears are fantasies about something that *could* happen in the future. Being present is inherently empowering. Your attention is focused where it ought to be — on the things you can affect. Being on a head-trip about things that may or may not ever happen is disempowering; your attention is on things you cannot affect.

Appreciation Is Healing

Most children get more criticism and control than appreciation. As a result, most adults have a fairly harsh inner critic unless they have had a lot of psychotherapy and learned to "re-parent" themselves.

When you offer sincere appreciation to someone about something she did or said or about one of her personal qualities, you are providing an antidote to any "poison" she may have been fed as a child. And if there are children in your life, this is the best time to begin offering your appreciations to them in generous doses.

In my work with people, I frequently encounter the client's inner judge or critic. This is the voice that tells the person things like, "People aren't interested in what you have to say"; "Don't try anything new unless you're absolutely sure you'll succeed"; and "You should never have opened your mouth! You really made a fool of yourself."

> The inner critic is a defense mechanism that attempts to keep us from getting into situations where we might get hurt. It's the voice that keeps us from testing our limits and expanding beyond them.

The inner critic is a defense mechanism that attempts to keep us from getting into situations where we might get hurt. It's the voice that keeps us from testing our limits and expanding beyond them.

My friend Heather had a strong fear of abandonment, stemming from a number of childhood incidents during which her mom had threatened to take her to the nearby orphanage and leave her there if she didn't stop asking for so much attention. This taught Heather that it was not safe to be too needy. It was better to rely on yourself.

Heather married Jack, a sensitive man who made his living as an artist and an inventor. Initially, he had been drawn to Heather for her independent spirit and her competence, but as their marriage matured, he began to get glimpses of another aspect — her soft, dependent side. He liked seeing more of this side of her. It gave him the opportunity to be there for her in ways that made him feel useful, powerful, and competent.

According to Heather, her ability to reveal her softer side grew out of the healing she experienced living for the past eight years with Jack. "Jack glows when I walk into the room. He tells me how beautiful I look and smell and how lucky he feels to be with someone whose touch feels so nourishing to him. I never could think of one positive thing about myself until I married him. He has been so good for me." I knew Heather before she met Jack, and I have witnessed the changes she's talking about. Before Jack, there was an aura of strength, yes, but it had an over-the-top quality to it. She appeared to be outrageously confident and at the same time always on guard. After meeting Jack, her self-confidence had more humility mixed with it. She seemed more relaxed in her speech and actions — as if her expressions were coming from a deeper place inside her.

From talking with her about her changes over the past eight years, I have learned that hearing Jack's appreciations on a daily basis has helped her connect to a part of herself she never knew existed. It's the part that really trusts that she is loveable, no matter what anyone else says to her or about her. Though Jack's positive statements are what helped her get in touch with this inner source of self-support, she knows that now, even if Jack were to die or leave, she will always have access to this part of herself.

Appreciation Expands Our Capacity for Pleasure

In working to help people live more authentically, I like to help them uncover the limiting beliefs that keep them from realizing who they really are. Perhaps the most common self-limiting personality trait of all is the arbitrary limit people place on how much goodness or pleasure they will allow into their lives. I believe we learned this limit at a very early age from our parents and our major cultural institutions like school, church, and work. Our cultural conditioning has taught us that we must work hard to earn money or grades, and then, when all our work is finished, we can allow ourselves a period of rest, fun, or self-indulgence — if there's ever time for it. Supporting this cultural conditioning is the inner critic, which has various ways of getting the message across that "You're not enough." By internalizing the "not enough" message, we make ourselves vulnerable to being manipulated by mass media, propaganda, and advertising, as well as by an extremely demanding work ethic. The result is we have little time or appetite for pleasure.

> Perhaps the most common self-limiting personality trait of all is the arbitrary limit people place on how much goodness or pleasure they will allow into their lives.

There is an invisible ceiling on most people's capacity for feeling good. Anxiety and depression are the mental illnesses of our age. And if we don't suffer from one of these, it's often because we have found some addictive substance or compulsive behavior to help us deal with our repressed pain over being trapped in a numb or tense body. Yet our potential is so much more than this.

I see the liberal use of face-to-face appreciation as one important antidote to our collective malaise. I have witnessed how sharing appreciations can change a depressed couple into a happy one. I have seen families transformed from tense to joyous after agreeing that every day they will each offer at least one appreciation to every other family member.

If you can find someone you know to share appreciations with on a daily basis, you'll see what I'm talking about. Just invite this person to agree to a daily ritual where you take turns sharing at least one appreciation each, using the form, "I appreciate you for..." (something specific that the other did, said, didn't do, or simply is).

I think you'll find that doing this is as good for the appreciator as it is for the one being appreciated. Appreciating others gets you in the habit of noticing more and more things to appreciate, thus leading to an overall attitude of gratitude for your life. Developing this attitude will create a sort of backdrop of positive feelings from which other feelings come and go. When you strengthen your appreciation muscles, you expand your overall capacity for experiencing life to the fullest.

> Appreciating others gets you in the habit of noticing more and more things to appreciate, thus leading to an overall attitude of gratitude for your life.

Appreciating Your Teenager

The teen years can be a tough time for the parent-child relationship. Teens often want a lot of autonomy but do not yet have the life experience needed to make good decisions. Teens want to be trusted. Parents can't help but worry.

One of the things teens most need is a realistic picture of their strengths and limits. But teens and parents tend to get polarized, with the teen trying to convince the parent of his strengths, and the parent trying to get the teen to recognize his limitations. I have helped many families communicate more effectively around this issue.

The Fowlers were a single parent family — dad and three children. Ed, the eldest, was "sixteen, going on twenty-five," according to his dad, Bryan. Bryan was a police lieutenant in town. In this line of work, he had seen many situations where teens got themselves in trouble due to poor judgment. Ed was a bright young man with a great sense of humor and an extroverted personality. He also had a large measure of impulsivity, which manifested in a number of ways, such as his falling in love quickly, having a hot temper on the road, and spending money on things he didn't need. As one might imagine, it was easy for Bryan and Ed to get into power struggles around the issue of Ed's need for freedom and Bryan's need to see some signs of caution and self-discipline.

> Teens and parents tend to get polarized, with the teen trying to convince the parent of his strengths, and the parent trying to get the teen to recognize his limitations.

During one session when Bryan and I were alone, I asked him to make a list of all the things his son had done, said, or accomplished over the past year that helped Bryan feel more trusting of Ed's ability to manage his life. After reading the list over, Bryan decided that he would like to tell Ed these things — delivering each appreciation in concrete language. Doing this was a relief from all the nagging he'd been doing lately. He thought it might feel better to say something positive to Ed for a change.

The next time I saw Bryan, he told me he had shared his

list of appreciations with Ed and had thereafter continued to add to the list, expressing new appreciations almost daily as they occurred to him.

Then, about a month later, Bryan told me that something surprising was beginning to happen with his son. Ed was staying home more in the evenings, appearing to enjoy just being around the family. And he and his dad had spent a few evenings together talking — something that had not happened in several years. But the biggest surprise was the fact that Ed was disclosing his self-doubts to Bryan and asking his dad for advice. He even shared that he was looking more carefully at his behavior with girls, noticing which of his actions added to his self-respect and which did not. In a word, Ed was taking more *responsibility* for managing his own life in a trustworthy manner.

What happened between father and son to bring about such a change? I imagine the change came in great measure from the fact that Bryan was criticizing less and appreciating more — thus getting himself out of the role of "cop" in his son's life. Once Bryan let go of that role, Ed moved in to fill the vacuum, becoming his own cop.

I think also that Ed needed to have his strengths mirrored back to him in specific terms by someone important to him. Like most of us, he needed external validation to help him connect with his ability to be self-validating. His self-esteem had been eroded by criticism and control. To deal with his anxiety about this shaky sense of self, he had been using drinking, driving, and sex as his painkillers.

The last time I saw Ed and Bryan together was very moving to me. Ed expressed appreciation for his dad. It went something like this: "I appreciate you, Dad, for making that list of the things you appreciate about me. I appreciate you for keeping on adding things to that list. And I appreciate you for telling me some of those things more than once. The first time you told me those things, I couldn't remember anything you said by the next day. Guess I was in shock. But after a while I got used to hearing it, and I started to believe you. Thanks, Dad, for helping me feel better about myself."

Appreciation Is Reinforcing

Appreciation is a powerful tool for creating what you want. According to ancient metaphysical wisdom (as well as modern learning theory), anything you appreciate or give positive attention to will increase, endure, or come into being. For this reason, it's wonderful to combine this key phrase with the key phrase, "I want. . . ." Your message begins with appreciating something the person is doing already before you request something additional. Here's how that would look: "Darling, I love how you've been stroking my belly. I want to feel your hands move up toward my breasts now."

Psychologists who study how people learn have proven that when you appreciate something someone does, this reinforces that behavior, making it more likely that the person will repeat this behavior in the future. So remember this when talking to your kids. Most parents and teachers already know that reward works a lot better than punishment to instill new habits. The important question is: how often do we remember to do this?

Appreciation as a Lifestyle

If you will integrate the phrase "I appreciate you for..." into your lifestyle — making it a valued part of your daily communications — it will change how you experience life. If we humans are here on Earth to help one another learn, grow, and heal, as I believe we are, then daily appreciations are a powerful aid in this process. If we can support ourselves and others in raising the bar for how much goodness we can all experience, the world cannot help but become a better place.

> If we can support ourselves and others in raising the bar for how much goodness we can all experience, the world cannot help but become a better place.

6

I HEAR YOU, AND I HAVE A DIFFERENT PERSPECTIVE

*I hear that you want to spend the weekend with your parents,
and I'd prefer that we spend a romantic weekend alone.
I hear you saying you want to get a new truck,
and I'm afraid we won't be able to make the payments.
I hear that you want to start being sexually open
to other lovers, and I still want to be monogamous.
I hear you saying you think we should forbid Suzie from
going out with boys until she is sixteen,
and I'm afraid she'll just do it behind our backs.*

It can be scary when someone you care about disagrees with you. Most of us prefer harmony to conflict. But if you've ever been in an emotionally engaging relationship, you probably realize that life without conflict is an impossible dream. No two people are going to want exactly the same thing at all times.

The good news is that it is possible to embrace your differences in a way that doesn't threaten your connection and in fact deepens it. Using the key phrase "I hear you, and I have a different perspective" will help you learn to honor both people's values, needs, or positions simultaneously.

Ron felt panicky every time his wife Rose stated an opinion that differed from his. As CEO of a very successful mid-size company, he wasn't used to feeling intimidated by disagreement, but with Rose it felt different. In his work life, he was used to telling people what he wanted and having them agree. Noting the discrepancy between how he felt at home and at work he couldn't help but wonder, "Have I always been afraid of conflict? Is that why I made sure I got to the top of the corporate ladder?" With this question in mind, he sought the help of a Getting Real coach, hoping to learn more about practicing the truth skill "Holding Differences."

> No two people are going to want exactly the same thing at all times.

During coaching sessions he found that he had always operated on the assumption that in a conflict situation, you have basically two choices: you get others to agree with you or you give in. It never occurred to him that he might hold in mind two seemingly opposing views — that he could listen openly to someone who disagreed with him without this threatening his own viewpoint. To help him get a felt experience of this new insight, I asked him to invite Rose into a session with us.

At the time of our session, he and Rose were in disagreement about how to handle the fact that their twenty-five-year-old son, Peter, was still living at home, didn't have a job, and didn't seem motivated to live independently from his parents. Rose thought they should tell Peter that he could no longer live with them; they would let him stay one more month, and then he was out. Ron felt worried that Peter would wind up on the streets selling drugs. As their coach, it was not my intent to solve the problem about Peter so much as to give them tools to resolve this conflict as well as future conflicts.

I asked Rose to state her position and then asked Ron to respond using the phrase "I hear you, and I have a different perspective." Here's how that went:

ROSE: I am not willing to have Peter around anymore. I'm ready to tell him he has to leave our home.

RON: I hear you saying that you're ready to ask Peter to leave, and I have a different feeling about this.

Ron's words sounded strained and unconvincing, but it was a good start. I asked Rose to state another opinion so Ron could get more practice holding differences:

ROSE: I think he'll get a job if he has to. I don't think he'll wind up living out of a shopping cart.

RON: I hear that you think he'll get himself a job if he has to, and I have a different prediction.

After a few more such practice rounds, I asked Ron to elaborate on his disagreement with Rose's position. So in addition to using the one-sentence "I hear you, and I have a different perspective," he was encouraged to expand on his initial statement, as in, "I'm afraid he'll resort to sell-

> It never occurred to him that he could listen openly to someone who disagreed with him without this threatening his own viewpoint.

ing drugs. That's even worse than the shopping cart scenario."

He found it much less stressful to do this now that he had the idea that it was really okay to have a different view. He told us that using this key phrase was helping him feel less threatened by the fact that he and Rose disagreed. It showed him that their differences were not about one person being right and one being wrong. And the biggest insight of all was his discovery that as his fear of conflict lessened, his ability to be present with Rose increased. He was no longer defensive and guarded around her. Rose felt the shift and told him it helped her trust him more: "Now I'm not so worried that you're just trying to avoid a confrontation with Peter by taking the position you have taken. Before we learned this communication skill, I couldn't trust what you said about anything if it involved disagreeing with me. Now, I trust that you'll let me know how you really feel."

Holding Differences Supports Mutual Trust

The ability to be present to yourself and to another at the same time builds trust: it builds self-trust because you're no longer assuming that you'll lose yourself if you become open to the other's views; and it helps others trust you because they can sense that while you're really showing up for yourself, you care about their views as well.

If you cannot get to the point where you can sincerely speak the words "I hear you, and...," you will never be a very good negotiator. All relationships require frequent negotiations of one sort or another. People see things differently and want different things. It's a fact of life. And if you want your relationships to work, people need to feel that you are not just out for yourself, but that you care about their needs and views. Of course, you cannot allow yourself to be truly open to another's view if you're in fear of losing touch with your own. That's why this key phrase is so important. Holding differences is a rather advanced communication skill. But it is one that is going to become more and more useful as the world becomes more diverse, interconnected, and complex.

> You cannot allow yourself to be truly open to another's view if you're in fear of losing touch with your own.

Futurists tell us that the human brain is evolving at a rapid rate in this information age due to ever-accelerating change and increasing diversity. More and more people are realizing that things we used to think of as mutually exclusive are often quite compatible — when viewed from a broader perspective or "bigger mind."

Expanding Lifestyle Options for Partners

One of the ways that increasing change and complexity are affecting intimate relationships is the fact that partners are more aware of a variety of lifestyle options. Long-term monogamy is no longer the only acceptable form of relationship, for example.

Especially after their kids are grown, many divorced people are deciding to remain uncommitted and spend time with more than one intimate partner. Carol met Rand through an internet dating site. When she learned that he had been married for twenty-eight years to one woman and had raised three children, she assumed that he was looking for a family-oriented monogamous relationship, just as she was. In time, however, she found that he was not looking for a mate but rather wanted to remain autonomous and free to love as many women as he felt like loving. He had begun to feel trapped toward the end of his marriage and had vowed never to get into that situation again. By the time Carol realized this, she had already fallen in love with Rand.

She found herself in the predicament of wanting to have a monogamous, committed relationship with him, but because she loved him and really wanted him to be happy, she also wanted him to feel free to love whomever he wanted to love. The statement "I hear you, and I have a different perspective" became really important to her. She often found herself making statements like this: "I hear that you want to be sexual with others besides me, and I wish you felt differently. I wish you wanted to be exclusively with me"; "I want you to only make love with me, and I want you to have what you want — which I know is to have a number of lovers. This is difficult for me to hold, and I love you so I'm choosing to stay as long as you want me to"; "I want to be fully open and vulnerable with you, and I can't seem to stay as open as I'd like because of your lifestyle choice."

Stating things in "both/and" terms can help you deal with the differences associated with loving someone who wants a different sort of relationship than you do. Can you see how this key phrase helps Carol articulate and make sense of her dilemma? She wants him to have what he wants, and at the same time, she wants what she wants. She wants to feel safe and open with him, and at the same time she wants to protect herself by not overcommitting to him, given his limited availability to her.

If you were Carol, can you imagine how you might experience such a predicament? Can you imagine feeling those two contradictory things at once: the wish to have what you want alongside the wish for your partner to have what he or she wants? Some people can't stand the tension, so they jump to a premature decision like "I'm out of here." Yet sometimes when you do stay with your experience of the two sides of the paradox, you get to a deeper level of what the conflict is really about. It can be intensely painful, but I have found that if you can embrace your pain with awareness, a breakthrough will often occur.

> Can you imagine feeling two contradictory things at once: the wish to have what you want alongside the wish for your partner to have what he or she wants? Some people can't stand the tension, so they jump to a premature decision.

The secret to staying in the impasse is using this key phrase as a kind of mantra to help you hold your differences and "hold" or contain the pain of being frustrated. It's so easy to blame, give in, or run. But none of these options are truly self-respecting. The most self-respecting way to be with differences with a loved one is to respect and honor your own position while at the same time respecting your partner's right to want something different.

In Carol's case, using this key statement to help her mentally embrace the two poles at once seemed to stretch her capacity for relating. Clearly she was not in control of this one. Each day of holding differences showed her new feelings and needs, new vulnerabilities, and new levels of acceptance of things she could not change. When she and Rand had begun, she had envisioned finding love from a devoted other. Instead she found a capacity for love inside herself that went far beyond anything she had ever experienced. After much pain and difficulty she finally arrived at that "big mind" perspective.

> Each day of holding differences showed her new feelings and needs, new vulnerabilities, and new levels of acceptance of things she could not change.

I realize that hanging out in such painful circumstances may seem intolerable to most readers, but if a person can do this for long enough, without harming her health, she will be changed by the experience. This change is not predictable. It doesn't take the form of giving in or compromising but rather of expanding oneself. In my thirty-five years as a counselor and coach, I have come to trust the expansion that occurs when you make it a regular practice to say and to feel, "I hear what you want, and I want something different."

Using This Statement
When You Feel Misunderstood

A difficult situation for most of us is one where someone challenges you about something you've said, but you know you never said those words. They have misinterpreted or misunderstood you. After sharing a large delicious meal together, Al asked Leslie, "Are you having dessert?" Later on that evening, as the pair was getting dressed to go out to a movie, Leslie confronted him with, "...and I didn't like you telling me I was eating too much!" Al was stunned and, for a moment, speechless. Then he remembered the key phrase we're learning here, so he replied, "I hear you saying you didn't like my telling you that you were eating too much, and I have a different recollection of what happened." Just having this statement ready in his repertoire helped him stay present and nonreactive. It grounded him in the reality that she heard one thing while he recalled saying a different thing. Can you see how using this key phrase gets things started on a more even keel?

> Just having this statement ready in his repertoire helped him stay present and nonreactive.

Having said this, Al can now elaborate on his memory of the conversation. He might even choose to employ some version of one of the other seven key phrases at this point, such as, "As I say this, I notice I'm getting defensive" or "Hearing you say that, I feel upset." These statements bring him more in touch with his own bodily feelings. This has the effect of helping him feel connected to himself and to Leslie. It will probably also help her feel more connected to him. When you drop into a state of present-centered awareness, other people tend to feel more connected to you.

She Wants to Talk Now and He Wants to Do It Later

Here's a tough situation that many couples experience: One of you wants to talk about the argument you just had right away so you can get it resolved. The other needs time to cool down or collect himself. If you're the one who wants to do it now, you probably feel a fair degree of urgency. Can you imagine putting out your request, hearing the other say, "Not now," and responding with, "I hear you say you don't want to talk about it now, and I feel strongly that I want to do it right away"? Can you imagine how that might shift your consciousness from pain over your own frustration to holding a larger perspective — the pain of feeling this difference between you?

The ability to shift into a bigger mind is a very advanced relationship skill. You are not in any way abandoning your own needs. What you are doing is including *more* in your point of view. Holding a more expanded point of view fosters a deeper sense of connection with others. It also supports a higher level of creative problem solving — because it promotes cooperation instead of competitiveness. When two people have a problem, the best, most lasting and viable solution is the one that grows out of both people's participation. Using the phrase "I hear you, and…" affirms the reality and validity of both views, while at the same time giving partners a structure for containing the pain that the difference causes. When you use this statement, it shows your partner that you are feeling pain over the discrepancy between his wants and your own. It connects you with his pain about that very same discrepancy. So, in essence, it is a shared experience of pain. Shared pain about something significant can bring partners closer together — even as they mourn the fact of their differences.

This statement also helps partners feel seen and heard. When partners feel seen, heard, and moved by the other, new creative energy gets released that had been tied up in the conflict. Using this key statement affirms that there is space for two points of view,

> The ability to shift into a bigger mind is a very advanced relationship skill.

not just one, in this relationship. This makes the relationship feel more spacious.

How This Statement Fosters Presence

Any time you are attached to getting your own way, you're probably in a state of fear. When your mind is on some feared future outcome, you're not present. This key phrase helps you get present by embracing the reality that you and your partner have differing perceptions or needs. It helps you consider and attend to more of the total reality of your current situation. The ability to see and feel more, without shutting down around the things you wish were not so, brings you more present. It's like affirming that you have the capacity to hold a view of your differences that is inclusive of both partners' needs.

7 | CAN WE TALK ABOUT HOW WE'RE FEELING?

*How are you feeling about this
relationship? Is it meeting your needs?
Can we talk about how we're feeling about what's going on?
I'd like to talk about what just happened. I think
we may be stuck in a pattern.
Can we talk about what's happening?
Before we leap into having sex tonight,
I want to check in with you about how we're both feeling.*

The ability to step back from an interaction and check in with yourself or reflect on what's going on is a skill that you need if you want to have successful relationships. This chapter will give you a doorway into such a conversation.

"Can we talk about how we're feeling?" can be used to get you communicating about something that just happened a minute ago, or it can prompt you to step back and look at how satisfied you are in this relationship overall. If you learn to use this statement regularly, you'll have what you need to stay connected to yourself and to your partner. Checking in with each other helps you keep your actions in tune with your ever-changing feelings and needs. It will keep your relationship from getting stagnant.

Meeting the Challenge of Change

We all know that the forces of change and uncertainty affect our careers and our livelihoods, but we often minimize how the rapidly changing cultural landscape affects relationships. Every day, through the media and the internet, we are bombarded with information about new lifestyle options and self-improvement methods. The media and advertising titillate us constantly with "new and better" ways to be and to live. An even more significant factor that complicates today's relationships is the fact that social attitudes toward marriage and partnership have changed such that people now feel much more permission to be single, to play the field, or to change partners when the going gets rough.

If your partner is feeling dissatisfied with something about your present situation and wants it to change, you need to hear this so the two of you can keep on growing and developing your relationship. This is where "Can we talk...?" comes in. It is a way for partners to constantly give feedback to each other, so the course of the relationship can be corrected if need be.

> "Can we talk...?" is a way for partners to constantly give feedback to each other, so the course of the relationship can be corrected if need be.

When I speak about learning and changing in a relationship, I am referring mainly to the moment-to-moment minor adaptations that we all need to be making all the time in the relationship dance. People's needs for closeness vs. distance change not only from day to day, but from moment to moment. Every interaction you have with a partner is like a dance in which one person takes a step and then the other either follows that lead, leads the dance in a different direction, or resists. "Can we talk...?" helps you stop and tune into the subtler movements of the dance between two people. It's like taking a time-out to sense and feel more of what's inside of you and between you. I often say that living a conscious life is like surfing a wave. Like a surfer on an ocean wave, you need to be in constant touch with the feedback you are receiving from your environment, your own body, and the others around you. This enables to you stay in balance with the many aspects of life that could wipe you out if you don't pay attention. This key phrase helps you pay attention to what's going on in and around you.

Checking In during Lovemaking

Brad and Molly had been dating for two months and had gotten to the heavy petting stage in their lovemaking. As they were making out one night, Molly began to feel more sexually aroused than she had been in a very long time. Her thought was, "Wow! I really want to feel him inside of me now, but I don't know if our relationship is ready for this next stage of intimacy. I want it, but I'm afraid I may regret it tomorrow." When most new partners have a feeling like this, they keep it to themselves. They do not consider that this might be a perfect time to stop the action and check in with each other. Instead they go on automatic, numb themselves, and continue doing whatever they imagine is expected of them. As we know, when people withhold what they're thinking and feeling, they are no longer present.

Molly did something different. She touched Brad's face

and moved toward him saying, "I need to let you know how I'm feeling right now. Can we take a moment to check in?" Brad was responsive to her request. The conversation that followed went something like this: Molly confessed that although she was very turned-on, she was not feeling safe enough to go all the way. Brad followed her disclosure with one of his own, using the key phrase we learned in chapter 1, "Hearing you say you're turned-on but not feeling safe, I feel very close to you right now. Thank you." Then, he let her know that he, too, did not feel ready to have intercourse that night because he was feeling shy and a little tired. He also mentioned that he had been afraid to bring the topic up for fear of disappointing her. All of this took place in less than two minutes. After this brief interruption, they both felt a lot closer.

> "I need to let you know how I'm feeling right now. Can we take a moment to check in?"

Most partners do not think to check in at important times such as when they're getting to know each other sexually. So they usually wind up doing the expected thing instead of being honest about what's real and present. Partners may fear that the relationship isn't strong enough to hold the differences between two very unique individuals. Practicing this key phrase helps you develop the confidence to talk openly about your unique needs and preferences.

It is common for partners in both love and work to avoid facing and expressing anything that could bring up conflict or disagreement. It's easy to get into the habit of denying or glossing over anything potentially threatening to relationship harmony. When you get into the habit of checking in regularly, you learn to handle differences and conflicts before they have a chance to build up into something insurmountable. You learn to deal with frequent incremental changes instead of waiting for a crisis. You learn to surf the waves of change so you are less likely to get knocked down or wiped out by something unexpected.

> When you get into the habit of checking in regularly, you learn to handle differences and conflicts before they have a chance to build up into something insurmountable.

I see too many situations where a relationship will end with words like, "I've never been satisfied with our lovemaking," "You never knew how to give me a blow job," or "I've been feeling angry at you for months." Frequent check-ins can prevent such unwanted surprises. The conscious use of this key phrase helps us break the bad habit most people have of waiting for a crisis before they pay attention to a problem. This key phrase helps partners step back from, reflect on, and deal with the small problems or small frustrations as they come up — before they build up into a wall. It helps us notice the early warning signs that indicate the need for change.

In relationships as in life, change is the only constant. So why do we have so much difficulty embracing the need for moment-to-moment course correction in relating with others? I think the answer has something to do with our outdated notions about change. Most of us still see stability as the norm and change as a problem. We like things to be predictable — "no surprises." In reality, people's feelings and wants change constantly. As long as we resist this fact, we will

Most of us still see stability as the norm and change as a problem. We like things to be predictable — "no surprises." In reality, people's feelings and wants change constantly. As long as we resist this fact, we will not learn the very important lesson of how to allow for constant change within an ongoing relationship.

not learn the very important lesson of how to allow for constant change within an ongoing relationship. The ability to embrace change in the context of long-term stability is one of the biggest relationship challenges of our time. "Can we talk...?" will help you develop this important skill.

Checking In during an Argument

"Can we talk...?" is a way to step a few feet back from an intense interaction while it is happening. It gives partners a structure for expressing their in-the-moment feelings about what they have just been doing or talking about.

Julia and Russell had been dating for eight months and were having frequent and painful discussions regarding scheduling time to be together. She wanted more evenings and weekends together, but since he was involved in starting a new business, he felt he could not be available that much. As their voices became louder and their language more hard-edged, it was apparent they were both quite attached to their positions. Feeling frustrated and helpless, Julia decided to try something she had never done before. She asked Russell, "Can we push 'pause' for a few minutes and look at what we're feeling?" Russell seemed not to hear her at first, and when he finally did look up at her, his words "What's wrong now?" stunned her. She thought of retreating, and she almost backed off with her usual "Never mind." But something in her decided not to give up just yet. So she repeated her request, "I'm wishing we could step back for a few minutes and look at what we're feeling. Will you do this with me?" Hearing this, Russell seemed to calm down. It was as if he just needed a bit more time to shift gears. He hadn't been quite ready to drop his combative stance when he heard her first request. Now he softened a little and asked, "What did you have in mind?" In the conversation that followed, the pair took turns sharing feelings and self-talk about the fact that they had so much trouble coming to agreement:

JULIA: I want for us to talk about how we feel about what we've been doing. It feels like a familiar argument, and I'm tired of it. As I say this I feel very, very sad.

RUSSELL: I hate it that we can't agree on much of anything. I wish we weren't fighting like this.

JULIA: I'm sorry that I called you self-absorbed. I regret saying that. I was feeling helpless and unable to get your attention.

RUSSELL: When you called me self-absorbed, I wondered, "What's she really upset about? Is it really just that I have to work on weekends?"

JULIA: Well, right now what bothers me is how you've been treating me during this discussion. I see you not looking at me...like you can't stand to face me.

RUSSELL: I appreciate you for saying that. I've been feeling guilty about the stuff you're telling me. And I guess I wasn't admitting how angry I am. I just want so much for us to get along.

JULIA: Maybe we should stop trying to plan our schedule and talk about our resentments. I know when I have a lot of piled up anger, it's hard for me to listen or make sense. I just attack. I want to stop doing that.

RUSSELL: I'm sorry I called you a big baby. I was just angry. I vote that we take a break and clear the air of all this backed up anger before we get back to talking about our schedules.

JULIA: Thanks for saying that.

By stopping the action for a check-in, the pair saw that they had not been connecting with each other during the discussion about schedules. As they continued to share, they saw that the fact of this emotional disconnect was as frustrating as their disagreement over the issue. If they had not used "Can we talk...?" at that point, they might have continued for a lot longer hurling accusations at each other, without ever mentioning their true feelings. Checking in brought them into the here and now. As they continued from this point, they used another key phrase, "I have some (angry) feelings to clear with you." After revealing and clearing their anger, they could better hear each other's ideas about possible solutions to their scheduling problem.

The check-in allowed the couple to bring enough awareness to the interaction to see that they really needed to clear their anger before trying to solve a problem together.

The check-in allowed the couple to bring enough awareness to the interaction to see that they really needed to clear their anger before trying to solve a problem together.

Bringing Hidden Tensions into the Light

Toby and Tara were distressed by their four-year-old son's stubborn refusal to eat anything but bread and jelly. They argued often about how to encourage their precious boy to eat a healthier diet. One day as they were having a conversation about this, Tara's voice became loud and strident. Toby felt an old familiar feeling that "someone big and important is unhappy with me." But since he had a control pattern of overriding his fears and acting superior, he came back at his wife with, "You know you worry too much, so let's just have a nice day and deal with this the next time it comes up." This triggered Tara's fear that "people don't care about my feelings." She muttered, "We'll just do it your way again, eh?" Toby acted as if he didn't hear her. Accustomed to this reaction, Tara retreated into silence, wondering to herself how she could've married someone as insensitive as Toby.

To the untrained observer, this conversation may sound fairly benign. Without knowing the subtext going on under Toby and Tara's words, one might say that this conversation is rather typical for married couples. But the fact is that their home has such an air of chronic relationship tension that their four-year-old son is being affected by it. Trying to distract his parents from their problems, he unwittingly "decides" to give them something else to worry about — him and his food sensitivities.

Many families (and work teams too) have an atmosphere of constant tension — something that obviously takes its toll on people's creative energy. "Can we talk...?" is very helpful in bringing this tension to light so people can deal with it and make the necessary changes.

Whenever I notice this sort of tension in my own relationships or in those of my clients, I invite us to "stop the action" and reflect on how we are feeling and what we are saying to ourselves. Simply using a phrase like, "Let's take a look at how we're both feeling about what's going on," works very well.

The Need to Feel Connected

As Toby and Tara's relationship coach, I taught them to stop the action like this in the middle of their subtle but frequent power struggles. In time, they also learned to reflect on: "Let's look at what we're doing and whether 'what we're doing' is getting us what we want." After some success using this key phrase, Toby and Tara came to the realization that whatever argument was going on, it was always about the same thing — Toby's need to avoid feeling scolded and Tara's need to feel heard. And underlying these needs was their deeper need to feel connected to each other. As we saw in the example above with Julia and Russell, the feeling of disconnection is often at the root of partners' frustrations. People will argue and try to change each other in an attempt to get their partner to be more like them (or to love them in a particular way) instead of simply feeling the pain of their differences or the frustration of not being in

> Toby and Tara came to the realization that whatever argument was going on, it was always about the same thing — Toby's need to avoid feeling scolded and Tara's need to feel heard. And underlying these needs was their deeper need to feel connected to each other.

harmony. If they would stop and simply feel whatever they feel, instead of thinking their partner should be different, the two partners might naturally feel closer. It is not true that two people must have similar needs and styles in order to feel connected, but many people get off on that track — trying to change the partner, instead of feeling how it feels to have differences. Sharing your frustrations about your differences can be a bonding experience of sorts. You're both feeling something similar in that you both wish for more harmony. Checking in gets you into your feelings and off of your positions.

> Sharing your frustrations about your differences can be a bonding experience of sorts. You're both feeling something similar in that you both wish for more harmony. Checking in gets you into your feelings and off of your positions.

Once Toby and Tara heard each other speak about their frustrated desire to feel connected, that, in itself, was a big first step toward harmony. When two people step back and look at their predicament together, the energy shifts from adversarial to cooperative. In the case of this couple, their four-year-old son's eating problems cleared up as soon as their tensions were aired and dealt with. This is what usually happens. Buried conflict leads to unconscious "acting out." Resolving these tensions brings the whole system back into harmony.

Connecting with Our Wants

"Let's look at what we're doing" helps two people get in touch with their wants. The simple act of stepping back to see the bigger picture allows us to see where we are now, where we want to be, and what we're doing to try to satisfy our wants. Usually we find that it's the "what we're doing" piece that needs to change. In the situation with Toby and Tara, they needed to allow themselves to fully experience the pain of not feeling more in synch. Toby found that he relaxed as soon as he heard Tara talk about her wish to feel heard. Likewise, Tara opened up and let down her guard as she heard Toby admit his need to feel appreciated by her. In Julia and Russell's case, they both needed to clear some anger before getting back to the task of working out their schedules.

Whenever you use this key phrase to help you step back from what's happening, you are likely to end up feeling more connected — because you are looking *together* at what's going on. This is already a big change in "what you're doing." What you *were* doing, arguing, has changed. Now, what you're doing is something much friendlier.

> Whenever you use this key phrase to help you step back from what's happening, you are likely to end up feeling more connected — because you are looking together at what's going on.

Are We Losing Ourselves to the Relationship?

Sarah and Jay were getting ready to celebrate their sixth wedding anniversary. They decided to make a community ritual out of the occasion — to invite their friends to a ceremony where they would dress up as they did on their wedding day and renew their vows. One evening as they were thinking together about what their vows had been the first time, Sarah started another kind of conversation: "I'm remembering the way we promised to love, honor, and obey six years ago. For these next six, I think I'd rather have you obey me less and love me more." This remark stunned Jay, so he used the key phrase of this chapter to bring things back to presence: "Ohhhh-kay, I'd like to talk about where that remark came from. Can we step back from what we're doing and talk about this?" As they talked together about what was going on between them at the subconscious level, they both revealed in turn that they were feeling cramped and controlled in the marriage. The love was dying from their trying too hard to "be a good partner" to each other. They were losing themselves in this relationship. After uncovering this problem, they were able to redefine their vows in a way that led to more permission and less obligation.

> When there is a buried conflict that has not been resolved, it is common for couples to throw subtle barbs or "zingers" at each other. Most couples just ignore these communications or at least pretend not to notice.

When there is a buried conflict that has not been resolved, it is common for couples to throw subtle barbs or "zingers" at each other. Most couples just ignore these communications or at least pretend not to notice. But Jay was aware enough to say what's real: "I'd like to talk." His skillful use of this statement was a major turning point in the relationship. As a result of this conversation, they renewed their vows wholeheartedly in a way that acknowledged and affirmed their individual differences.

The Thrill Is Gone

Gwen and Paul are engaged to be married, but she has the suspicion that he no longer enjoys making love to her. As evidence of this she points to the fact that he no longer looks into her eyes during lovemaking.

A situation like this is a good time to ask for a check-in. If she were to do this during lovemaking, she might ask, "Before we keep going here, could we push 'pause'? Could you just hold me for a minute while we talk about how we're feeling?" Many people have a belief that you shouldn't try to talk about such things while making love — that only pillow talk or sweet talk are acceptable here. But the reality is that people often have other things on their minds during lovemaking, and it's futile to pretend otherwise. If something is on your mind, and you're withholding speaking about it, you're not going to be very present to your lover. The best thing (and ultimately the sexiest thing) you can do is to be where you are and let your partner in on where you are. Often, after partners check in like this, they're more able to feel and express their passion.

When Gwen did this, what she learned was that Paul had been building up resentment inside himself about all the ways he'd been giving in to her regarding wedding plans and decisions. He felt relieved to find that she was truly interested in his opinions. She had simply been assuming that, because he was usually so assertive, he would let her know how he felt about her ideas. So after a rather long "pause" to clear the air, the two got back to making love and enjoying deeply satisfying eye-gazing.

When Your Partner Seems Distracted

Marti and Ti were discussing where to go on vacation when Ti noticed that she seemed distracted. He interrupted the conversation: "Marti, can we talk about something I'm observing here as we're talking?" When she agreed, he continued, "As I was just showing you the article about this new condo village, you were cleaning your fingernails. I'm imagining that behavior means you're not really interested in what I'm saying. Could you tell me what's going on for you?"

After this opening, Marti took some time to really look at how she had been feeling during the conversation. What she discovered was that she'd been "trying to be polite and not interrupt," when in fact she had something to talk about that she thought was much more pressing — the fact that her boss had just talked to her that day about a possible downsizing of the workforce. She realized she was also feeling envious of Ti's ability to make a living drawing cartoons, and that he got paid well for doing something he loved, while she was stuck in a job she hated.

After using "Can we talk. . .?" to get at what's going on now for each person, it is a short step to also using the key phrase, "I have some feelings to clear with you." In this case, Marti was able to clear her feelings of envy for how easily Ti makes money.

From this experience they learned that it's hard to be present to your partner when you're trying to act interested by pushing aside your real feelings. Once you express what's calling your attention, then your attention is really free to attend to your partner.

Using Check-ins for Work and Community Groups

Have you ever been in a group where a few people are doing all the talking while the others sit silently? What if you were to say, "Let's look at what we're doing," or "Let's take a moment to all check in about how we're feeling." Can you imagine this? This would instantly bring the whole group into the conversation.

> Have you ever been in a group where a few people are doing all the talking while the others sit silently? What if you were to say, "Let's look at what we're doing."

When I have done this, I'll say something like, "I'd like to stop the action for a minute and look at how this group is going. I'm curious especially about what Betsy and Bernie have to say." (Betsy and Bernie were the two quietest members.) Then, as we all consider "how it's going" together, several people usually mention the unbalanced participation before I do. From there, any number of solutions are possible. Most groups come to the conclusion that the more active members should try being quieter for a while — to give space for the less assertive members — and that usually works. What happens is that everyone gets to see how much the more silent members really had to say. They were just waiting for an opening!

Another good time to do a check-in is in a business meeting where you want to be sure that people don't leave with unexpressed resentment about how a decision was arrived at, or resistance to the course of action the group decided on. In this situation the group leader, or anyone who has the idea, will suggest that the business part of the meeting end ten or fifteen minutes early so you can all look together at how it went — what worked well and not so well, and what you'd like to do differently next time. When people have the idea that it's appropriate to speak about their leftover feelings, they usually do a pretty good job of expressing them. All it takes is the invitation to do so.

Groups who do this are more cohesive because they have a chance to express their frustrations and be heard rather than venting them in the corridors or restrooms afterward. Such groups are also able to learn from their experiences. In today's highly competitive organizations, groups and individuals need a way to look together at what they're doing and how they can improve things next time.

Can We Talk?

We have just seen how useful this statement can be, yet some people panic when they hear these words. For these people, this phrase (or something similar) is associated with past incidents where they felt criticized or belittled. So their defenses go up as soon as they hear it. Since so many people get tense just hearing the words "Can we talk?" try to be mindful of your attitude and tone when you use this statement. Don't say, "We need to talk." "We need to..." is a controlling way of saying, "I want to talk," or "Can we talk?" These latter two sentences are more relational and less manipulative. They allow space for the other to say no or "Not now."

As you get more fluent with this and the other six key phrases, you'll discover what works and doesn't work. Most people develop their own unique shorthand for the phrases they use most often — so this phrase might get shortened to something like "Check-in," or "Time-out."

However you say it, inviting someone you care about to help you understand him or her better is an act that builds trust. You're taking a risk in the interest of mutual understanding. Most people will appreciate you and support your effort.

8 | WORKING WITH THE SEVEN KEYS

These seven key phrases give you a script for improving your communication. They're easy to remember and easy to teach to others. They help you become more self-aware and more able to fully experience what is. They're like a template for becoming more conscious and intentional rather than blaming and passive. As such, they encourage a higher state of consciousness and self-responsibility.

When you have mastered all seven keys and their various applications, you pretty much have what you need to deal with the situations that drive most people apart — times when you feel hurt, angry, or misunderstood; when you have the impulse to run away, or to attack; when you are afraid to assert yourself or ask for what you want; when you feel stuck in a power struggle or a misunderstanding; and when you have said or done something that you regret.

Here, once again, are the seven keys, along with brief descriptions of how and where you might use each.

Key #1: Hearing You Say That, I Feel...

When someone gives you feedback, offers an opinion, or comments about any shared experience, you are likely to have a feeling response even if you are not aware of it. Your feeling response is very simple and basic. You might feel more open or more defensive, more relaxed or more tense, more attracted or more distant. Feeling statements are things like: I feel happy, I feel sad, I feel uncomfortable, I feel shut down, I feel turned-on, I feel connected to you, I feel fearful, I feel angry, and so forth.

Most of us are in the habit of bypassing our feelings much of the time and going straight to an attempt to manage the situation. We'll try to manage or control the outcome, our anxiety about an unknown outcome, or our own reactions. We offer advice, explain ourselves, make witty remarks, act more confident than we really feel, take charge, or tell a story. These are our habitual ways of managing our anxiety about not feeling in control.

> Most of us are in the habit of bypassing our feelings much of the time and going straight to an attempt to manage the situation.

When you simply state your feeling response, you are not doing any of these things. You are relating to the situation just as it is — not trying to manage or control anything. You accept the things you cannot control. You are open in your listening and open in your self-expression.

Using Key #1 keeps you present and connected to what just took place or what the other person just said to you. It helps you stay in the here and now and keeps you "on your own side of the net." Being on your own side of the net is a metaphor for talking about *your own* feelings and thoughts — rather than your assessments, judgments, or interpretations *about the other person,* his motives, or the appropriateness of his actions. Judgments and interpretations about the other are a type of defense mechanism. They help us maintain the illusion that we are in control — that we know things that we actually cannot know, such as someone else's intentions or hidden feelings. All we can really know for sure is what we ourselves experience. Communication based on your own personal present-time experience is more grounded and connected, less "heady." "Hearing you say that, I feel..." keeps you more in your heart and less in your head.

Key #2: I Want...

This phrase is meant to be followed by something specific that you want in this moment, for example: I want to hold your hand, I want your feedback on the report I gave you, I want you to look into my eyes when we're talking, I want to make love with you. Too many people assume that others know their wants. This assumption is actually a self-protective mechanism. It helps us avoid feeling the vulnerability associated with asking for what we want.

Too many people assume that others know their wants. This assumption is actually a self-protective mechanism. It helps us avoid feeling the vulnerability associated with asking for what we want.

Asking for what you want in specific terms at a time when you actually feel the want is another way to bring yourself into more powerful contact with the other person. Like the first statement, this one also brings you more into the present. And, like the first, it is an act of showing up more vulnerable — vulnerable in the sense that you are revealing that the other's response is important to you. Remember, you are *revealing* a want, not *demanding* that you get it. When you ask for something in an open, nondemanding frame of mind, you realize that you might not get it, and this too allows you to feel your vulnerability to the other.

When you ask for what you want *at a time when you are actually feeling it,* the other can feel the clarity and energetic power of your contact. For this reason you are more likely to have your want fulfilled. And even if you do not, there is some satisfaction in just knowing you showed up for yourself by asking.

Key #3: I Have Some Feelings to Clear

This statement opens the way for you to resolve uncomfortable feelings or unfinished business with someone. Doing so enables the two of you to get over whatever old business you have and get back into present time with each other. As you probably know, when you harbor "withholds," you are not able to be fully present.

You probably have someone in your life with whom you have left things unresolved or incomplete. If you can bring yourself to at least begin the conversation by using this key phrase, it's a good first step to opening the topic up for discussion so it can eventually be put to rest.

Once you have gotten your first sentence out, I suggest you mention that your intent is to clear the air so the two of you can get back into harmony with each other (or get back into a productive working relationship, or whatever). You might also inquire about whether this is a good time for the other person. If your intent is to relate rather than to control, remember to first "knock on someone's door," rather than just barging in. It's important to let the other person participate in the decision about when and how to have such an important discussion.

Key #4: I'm Getting Triggered

We all get our buttons pushed sometimes. This key phrase helps you recover from those moments when you automatically react aggressively or defensively. It helps you accept that you are not always completely present and self-aware. It gives you a quick and easy way to get yourself back into present time after one of your unconscious fear buttons has been pushed.

When you have this key ready to put into practice whenever you overreact, you have a way of buying time to check in, get reconnected with yourself, and perhaps revise your earlier response.

Key #5: I Appreciate You for...

This phrase prompts you to express in specific terms your gratitude for something someone did or said. It lets someone know how her behavior impacted you. As such, it's also a great way to show the other how you like to be treated. And

it prompts you to celebrate the things you are grateful for —
even small things.

The best appreciations are those that are spoken in the moment, as you are feeling them. When someone says or does
something that you appreciate, tell her right then and there. This
brings the two of you into powerful, positive present-time contact.

Sharing appreciation also has a profound healing function in relationships. Most people, when they were children,
did not have their strengths mirrored back to them enough
by the adults in their lives.
Most of us still long to be
seen and acknowledged for
our gifts. When we appreciate each other as adults, we
help each other heal from the
wounds of this sort of childhood neglect.

> Most of us still long to be seen
> and acknowledged for our gifts.
> When we appreciate each other
> as adults, we help each other
> heal from the wounds of child-
> hood neglect.

Appreciation strengthens a relationship so it can better
withstand life's inevitable challenges. The relationship becomes a source of pleasure and love — both life-giving qualities. Sharing pleasure is a bonding experience.

Key #6: I Hear You, and I Have
a Different Perspective

This compound sentence is useful when two people have a
difference in needs or views. Many people fear differences.
They see them as a threat. But, if worked with consciously,
differences can help the relationship expand as a container for
meeting each individual's needs. This sentence helps people
center themselves in the reality that there are two points of

view going on in their discussion. It also sets the context for a win/win attitude — I want you to win, *and* I want myself to win. It helps partners learn to hang in there through the uncomfortable period of ambiguity that occurs while partners are working out their differences.

People need the support for agreeing to disagree that this sentence provides. But even more important, this statement gives you a structure for being open to the other's views without losing touch with your own. Often the very act of "holding differences" in this way leads to a genuine expansion of your ability to reconcile or synthesize apparent opposites. Perhaps one of you wants to buy a new car and the other does not want to spend the money. Instead of giving in or trying to get your way, stating what you want alongside what you think the other wants creates a cooperative mindset because you are starting out by acknowledging the other. When cooperative energy is present, this allows a more creative, mutually beneficial solution to emerge.

> If worked with consciously, differences can help the relationship expand as a container for meeting each individual's needs.

Partners tend to trust one another more, so they aren't keeping so much vital information hidden (as occurs in most adversarial negotiations). With more information out in the open, a more viable solution can be reached.

Key #7: Can We Talk about How We're Feeling?

If two people are going to learn from an experience, especially a painful or frustrating one, they need to be able to witness that experience. If an interaction has gone or is going badly, one member of the pair needs to take leadership and suggest that both people step back from the situation and get perspective. You could say something like, "Let's look at what we are doing to see if this is what we really want to be doing." For example, let's say you notice you and your friend getting stuck in an argument about who is right and who is wrong. You might feel frustration or a sense that you are going around in circles. As soon as you notice things going awry, you would use this sentence, inviting the other to reflect on the interaction with you. You might say, for example, "Can we take a look at what's happening? I'm feeling frustrated with this conversation. How about you?" That would be your lead-in to stepping back, "rewinding the tape," and looking together at what just happened to see if either of you would like to change anything. After a short period of shared reflection, it's a lot easier to start over.

> After a short period of shared reflection, it's a lot easier to start over.

People often get so caught up in reacting to what's happening that they forget to step outside of it or above it long enough to notice whether what they are doing is reflecting their true feelings or getting them what they want. When you know how to invite the other into a conversation about "What are we doing?" "Is it authentic?" and "Is it working?" you can reflect on your actions, learn from the experience, and alter your course.

Making the Seven Keys Yours

Now that you know these seven key phrases, the next step is to make them yours by practicing them with the significant people in your life. In most relationships, you can start using the seven keys right away without any special explanation. You don't even need to tell the other person or persons that you are trying something new. But if you want to develop a relationship into one where both people intentionally help each other become more aware and present, then it's a good idea to pass this book along to the other and explain that you would like to have a relationship where you communicate more consciously.

A few caveats are also in order: With some people, the phrase, "I'm getting triggered," could cause *them* to become triggered. If you imagine this might happen, explain the notion of triggers or buttons to the other and show them this book.

The other sentence that could get a reaction is, "I have some feelings to clear." Some people are not fluent in the language of feelings, and they feel awkward when you express yours. With such people, I recommend that you go ahead and express your feelings. Don't be too inhibited by your fears about the other's reaction. You can *care* about the other's reaction, but this is different. If it's an important relationship, it's your responsibility to keep yourself clear of unexpressed resentments even if your partner is not doing this work. Of course, one of your recurring resentments could be the fact that when you tell her your feelings, she says, "Are you done yet?" Certainly it can be difficult to keep doing this work when your partner is not, but what choice do you have? You

> Often, as you use these seven keys with the same person over a period of time, she'll see how safe and effective it is to do so and follow suit.

cannot force someone. All you can do is express your wants, and when they are consistently frustrated, express your frustration. And remember to stay on your own side of the net.

As long as you stay on your own side of the net when using these seven phrases, you are serving the relationship. Serving the relationship will often include doing things that the other feels uncomfortable with. Remember, the goal is not to keep your partner comfortable. The goal is aliveness, spontaneity, presence, and honesty. These are the things that make a relationship satisfying and strong.

Usually if you express yourself responsibly, with the goal of connecting rather than controlling, the other will not feel offended. He or she may feel uncomfortable, but this is different. If you take a risk and do something new on behalf of the relationship, the other will probably sense this and appreciate you for it. And often, as you use these seven keys with the same person over a period of time, she'll see how safe and effective it is to do so and follow suit.

> When people learn to converse this way, it affects the quality of their consciousness. In a very deep and subtle way, it teaches them to say yes to each moment just as it is.

In Each Moment

As I have emphasized, these key statements bring people back to the here and now. When people learn to converse this way, it affects the quality of their consciousness. In a very deep and subtle way, it teaches them to say yes to each moment just as it is.

Most of us have been conditioned to avoid the present moment. Somehow we seem to be more comfortable focusing our attention on "stories" about things that have *already happened* or *could happen.* The "already happeneds" and "could happens" of life are in the mind. They are not now. So in a very real sense, they are not real. When we allow our lives to be controlled by the mind's need to stay within a certain comfort zone, we miss most of what real life is all about. We miss the ever-changing, moment-by-moment "now."

> When we allow our lives to be controlled by the mind's need to stay within a certain comfort zone, we miss most of what real life is all about.

The reason these keys are essential for authentic communication and relationship success is that they guide you gently into the here-and-now, which is where the relationship is really happening. They help you frame your reality in present-time terms, since the present time is where you actually have sensations (like pleasure or pain), feel feelings (like love or anger), and take action (like moving toward or away).

If your relationship is taking place mostly in your mind, your actions will be based not on your real sensations and feelings, but on something you have inferred, assumed, or interpreted. The reason most relationships don't work as well as they could is that too many critical moments of relating take place in people's minds, instead of in their bodies and hearts. Using these seven key phrases brings energy and attention to your person-to-person, heart-to-heart contact. They focus your attention where it can do some good.

There is a saying from the ancient wisdom traditions, "Now is the moment of power." It is only in this moment that you can really do or feel anything. I invite you to be part of the emerging trend toward real, honest, here-and-now contact in relationships.

APPENDIX

RESOURCES TO SUPPORT PRESENT-CENTERED COMMUNICATION

I f you want to master the seven keys, you will need people to practice with who recognize the value of present-centered communication. In this appendix, you will find places where you can connect with like-minded people and resources to support you — such as books, games, audio programs, and the "Start Your Own Honesty Salon Kit."

Internet Discussion Board

If you want to get practice interacting with like-minded people through our internet discussion forum, go to www.truthindating.com and click on the link "Discussion Forum." Here you will find questions and responses from potential friends and practice partners, as well as from me on topics ranging from sex to child rearing to completing unfinished business with parents or ex-partners.

Teleclasses

A teleclass is a workshop that takes place over the phone. This is a great way to meet people from all over the world. I offer teleclasses on such topics as: applying the seven keys in love, sex, and marriage; taking the seven keys into the workplace; truth in dating; sexuality; overcoming fears of intimacy; conscious flirting; creating the life you want; and how to start your own Honesty Salon. A teleclass is like a telephone conference call and can be attended by any number of participants, although the ideal size is ten to twelve participants. Group interaction is encouraged so that people get a chance to practice their truth-telling skills. People all call into the same "bridge number" at an agreed-upon time — which means that class participants can call in from anywhere in the world. Often people have a "homework buddy" whom they call during the week between classes to complete various homework practice exercises.

To find a list of existing teleclasses, visit the web site www.susancampbell.com. You may also call and ask to set up a class on a particular topic that interests you or at a particular time that works for you.

Honesty Salons

An Honesty Salon or Honesty Circle is a small group experience in which the same six to twelve people meet regularly to practice present-centered communication using the seven keys and the "ten truth skills" described in this volume and the books *Getting Real* and *Truth in Dating*. This is another wonderful way to meet people and get to know how others see you. Groups meet at least once a month for two or three hours each session. One person agrees to be the facilitator. The facilitator is someone who has attended a Getting Real workshop or who has purchased and worked with the "Start Your Own Honesty Salon Kit." To purchase this do-it-yourself resource, go to www.truthindating.com and click on "Community."

Game Nights

Anyone can host a Getting Real game night or Truth in Dating game night in their home or at a nearby recreation center. All you need to do is purchase *The Getting Real Card Game* or *The Truth in Dating Card Game* (available at www.truthindating.com or www.susancampbell.com). The games come with instructions on how to facilitate the game. Playing one of these games offers a chance to deepen your connections with others and find out how others see you while practicing some vital communication skills.

Hosting a game night is fun, heartwarming, and a great way to practice present-centered communication. The instructions that come with each game provide guidelines for how to customize the game for your particular group. The ideal group size for such an event is six to fourteen people. If your group is larger, you could have several small groups going on at once.

Many singles organizations, conferences, and church groups have used one of these games as an icebreaker or mini-workshop. You may consult me about how to modify the games for larger group formats. I have used the game as a community-building activity for large professional conferences and for luxury cruises.

Workshops

Workshops are an excellent way to meet like-minded people. Myself and my team of Getting Real coaches offer workshops of one day to one week. The most popular topics are: Truth in Dating, Getting Real, The Couple's Journey, Getting Real with Your Children and Teens, and Awakening Through Relationships. I also offer trainings for corporations and small businesses on Honest Feedback, Communication Skills for Preventing and Resolving Conflict, Surfing Chaos, How to Build a Winning Team, Bringing Out the Best in People Who Bring Out the Worst in You, and Truth at Work. I have also created a Truth at Work card game that can be used by coaches or trainers to foster better communication in work groups. For details visit www.susancampbell.com, email drsusan@susancampbell.com, or call (707) 829-3646.

Singles Events

We offer a variety of get-acquainted events for singles. Like workshops, these events are a great way to meet and get to know other people who value authenticity. Some are sponsored by the Learning Annex in various cities such as New York, San Diego, and San Francisco. Most are sponsored by my company, Getting Real Resources. For details, visit www.susancampbell.com and www.truthindating.com under the link "Courses."

Become a Coach

Since the best way to learn something is to teach it, you may want to get trained to be a Getting Real coach or to lead Honesty Salons, game nights, or workshops that teach the seven keys. To learn more about coach training opportunities, visit www.susancampbell.com or call (707) 829-3646.

Online Community

You may join a free online email "discussion list" of people interested in applying the seven keys in their relationships. In this online forum, people ask questions and give one another feedback and counsel. Sometimes we also play a modified version of the Truth in Dating Card Game or the Getting Real Card Game online. To join this list, send a blank email with "subscribe" in the subject line to gettingreal-subscribe@ yahoogroups.com.

Free Online Newsletter

You may also subscribe to my free e-zine, *Truth in Dating, Sex, and Marriage,* designed to support people who want to make an inner paradigm shift from being right to being real. To subscribe, send a blank email with "subscribe" in the subject line to truthindatingloveandmarriage-subscribe@yahoogroups.com.

Books

The following books focus on honest, present-centered communication:

Blanton, Brad. *Practicing Radical Honesty: How to Complete the Past, Live in the Present, and Build a Future.* Stanley, VA: Sparrowhawk Publishing, 2000.

———. *Radical Honesty: How to Transform Your Life by Telling the Truth.* New York: Dell, 1996.

———. *Radical Parenting: Seven Steps to a Functional Family in a Dysfunctional World.* Stanley, VA: Sparrowhawk Publishing, 2003.

———. *The Truth-Tellers: Stories of Success by Honest People.* Stanley, VA: Sparrowhawk Publishing, 2004.

Campbell, Susan. *Beyond the Power Struggle: Dealing with Conflict in Love and Work.* San Luis Obispo, CA: Impact, 1980. (This title is out of print but available from the author at www.susancampbell.com.)

———. *The Couple's Journey: Intimacy as a Path to Wholeness.* San Luis Obispo, CA: Impact, 1980. (This title is out of print but available as an e-book or hard copy from the author at www.susancampbell.com.)

———. *From Chaos to Confidence: Survival Strategies for the New Workplace.* New York: Simon and Schuster, 1995.

————. *Getting Real: 10 Truth Skills You Need to Live an Authentic Life*. Novato, CA: New World Library, 2001.

————. *Truth in Dating: Finding Love by Getting Real*. Novato, CA: New World Library, 2004.

Covington, Stephanie, and Liana Beckett. *Leaving the Enchanted Forest: The Path from Relationship Addiction to Intimacy*. San Francisco: Harper and Row, 1988.

Deyo, Yaacov, and Sue Deyo. *Speed Dating*. New York: Harper Collins, 2002.

Dhiravamsa. *Turning to the Source: Using Insight Meditation and Psychotherapy for Personal Growth*. Nevada City, CA: Blue Dolphin Publishing, 1990.

Fisher, Bruce, and Robert Alberti. *Rebuilding: When Your Relationship Ends*. San Luis Obispo, CA: Impact Publishers, 2000.

Hendricks, Gay, and Kathlyn Hendricks. *Conscious Loving*. New York: Bantam, 1990.

————. *The Conscious Heart*. New York: Bantam, 1997.

Heumann, Suzie, and Susan Campbell. *The Everything Guide to Great Sex*. Holbrook, MA: Adams Media, 2003.

Kasl, Charlotte. *If the Buddha Dated*. New York: Penguin Putnam, 1999.

Lowe, Paul. *In Each Moment*. Vancouver, B.C.: Looking Glass Press, 1998.

Psaris, Jett, and Marlena Lyons. *Undefended Love*. Oakland, CA: New Harbinger Publications, 2000.

Tolle, Eckhart. *The Power of Now*. Novato, CA: New World Library, 1999.

Videotapes

Campbell, Susan. *The Couple's Journey: Intimacy as a Path to Wholeness.* A thirty-minute interview with Susan Campbell by Thinking Allowed host Jeffry Mishlove. Available at "Products," www.susancampbell.com.

————. *Getting Real: 10 Truth Skills You Need to Live an Authentic Life.* Two lively thirty-minute interviews with Susan Campbell by talk show host Asia Powers. Available at "Products," www.susancampbell.com.

————. *How to Build a Loving Relationship.* A one-hour self-help workshop covering the five key ingredients of a successful relationship. Available at "Products," www.susancampbell.com.

CRM Films. *Riding the Wave: Strategies for Change* (based on Susan Campbell's book about "surfing chaos," *From Chaos to Confidence: Survival Strategies for the New Workplace*). 17 minutes, 1999. Available from CRM Films at (800) 421-0833 or from "Products," www.susancampbell.com.

Audio Programs by Susan Campbell

Bringing Out the Best in People Who Bring Out the Worst in You. Tips for dealing with the people in your life who push your buttons.

The Do It Yourselves Sex Therapy and Enrichment Kit. Includes audio instructions and a self-paced workshop to assess where you'd like to be and help you get there, using the seven keys and ten truth skills.

Getting Real: Introduction to the 10 Truth Skills. A recorded
interview with New Dimensions Radio host Michael
Toms.

Getting Real: Relating More, Controlling Less. A recorded
speech about why we lie, sugarcoat and pretend, and
how to notice when you are controlling vs. relating.

A Guide to Open Communication. A discussion of the difference between communicating to "know and be known"
vs. communicating to get a certain result.

*How the 10 Getting Real Truth Skills Can Help You Navigate
the 20 Most Significant Challenges in Relationships.* A self-
help program for beginning, maintaining, and deepen-
ing relationships.

Overcoming the Fear of Intimacy. A discussion about why
people fear intimacy and how to build your capacity for
deeper connection with others.

What Can You Realistically Expect in a Relationship? A discussion of things you can expect that most relationship
counselors don't talk about.

Why Opposites Attract. A description of why we often attract
people who push our buttons. All of these audiotapes are
available at "Products," www.susancampbell.com.

B

THE SEVEN KEYS AT A GLANCE

ere is a list of the Seven Keys to Authentic Communication and Relationship Success that you can photocopy and put on your refrigerator or bedroom mirror.

Key #1: Hearing you say that, I feel...

Key #2: I want...

Key #3: I have some feelings to clear.

Key #4: I'm getting triggered.

Key #5: I appreciate you for...

Key #6: I hear you, and I have a different perspective.

Key #7: Can we talk about how we're feeling?

ACKNOWLEDGMENTS

The works of Fritz Perls, Carl Jung, Brad Blanton, and Paul Lowe have contributed much to my own work, and I am grateful to have been influenced by their hearts and minds. Thanks also to the members of the five ongoing Honesty Salons that I host in the San Francisco Bay Area. Some of these truth-seekers have been working with me in this format for eight years. Their willingness to adventure to the deepest levels of authenticity and transparency has been inspiring, instructive, and enriching. They have been both my own support group and my main laboratory for field testing the tools presented in this book.

Special thanks to Randy Mack and Dean LaCoe for their careful reading of the manuscript, and to my best girlfriend,

Peller Marion, for her constant encouragement and humor. I am grateful also to my publisher, Linda Kramer, who conceived of the idea for this book, to New World Library's Marketing Director, Munro Magruder, who thought of the title, and to my editor, Georgia Hughes.

INDEX

ABOUT THE AUTHOR

Susan Campbell has been a relationship coach, speaker, and workshop leader for thirty-five years and has written eight previous books on interpersonal relationships. She is also the creator and publisher of five entertaining and educational card games for children, teens, adults, couples, work teams, and singles, as well as one for birthday parties. All of her games promote more authentic relating among players.

Susan has appeared on numerous talk shows, including CNN's *NewsNight, Good Morning America,* and *The Dr. Dean Edell Show,* and she has been published widely in popular magazines.

Her Learning/Discovery approach to communication, conflict, and change is the subject of a twenty-minute professional training video produced and distributed by CRM

Films. Based on her book, *From Chaos to Confidence: Survival Strategies for the New Workplace,* the film and accompanying workbook are widely used by Fortune 500 companies and government agencies. As an internationally known professional speaker, Susan speaks on such topics as Surfing Chaos, Honest Feedback in the Workplace, Coping with Constant Change, How to Build a Winning Team, and Successful Win-Win Negotiating. She publishes a newsletter entitled *Truth in Dating, Sex, and Marriage,* which she offers free to clients and former clients.

Susan leads public seminars throughout the country and in Europe on Getting Real, Truth in Dating, Truth at Work, and The Couple's Journey: Relationship as a Path to Awakening. For information on her events, card games, or do-it-yourself relationship enrichment kits, call (707) 829-3646 or visit www.susancampbell.com.

H J Kramer and New World Library is dedicated to
publishing books and audio products
that inspire and challenge us to improve
the quality of our lives and our world.

Our products are available
in bookstores everywhere.
For our catalog, please contact:

New World Library
14 Pamaron Way
Novato, California 94949

Phone: (415) 884-2100 or (800) 972-6657
Catalog requests: Ext. 50
Orders: Ext. 52
Fax: (415) 884-2199

E-mail: escort@newworldlibrary.com
Website: www.newworldlibrary.com